Table of Contents

Table of Contents 1
Introduction 3
.... 4

The Hidden Word

Psalm 119:11

Exploring the Secrets of the Heart

by

Jaison Ndlovu

Copyright © 2024 Jaison Ndlovu All rights reserved.

DEDICATION

To my daughter, Lomalinda Grannie Ndhlovu, whose inspiring idea ignited this journey. To my sons Logic Amos, Eureka Eulogy, Russell Hillary and Elisha Heritage, not forgetting their sister, Misery, whose unwavering support and material assistance fueled its progression. To my spouse, Susan Ndlovu (nee Mahogo), whose genuine interest provided constant motivation. And to my dear mother, Resiya Magundwane, (nee Chikwinya), whose prayers guided every word written. To my grandchildren who I have always wanted to know and tell when I am gone. Last but not least, all my relatives. This book is a testament to the love, encouragement, and unity that has always surrounded me.

90

Introduction

"The Hidden Word: Exploring the Secrets of the Heart" by Jaison Ndlovu is a profound exploration of the Bible's intricate complexity and depth. This book delves into the concept of internalizing God's Word, as expressed in Psalm 119:11, and finds additional clarity and meaning in the context of John 1:1-5. Ndlovu examines the term "In the Beginning" (Berēshîth) in John 1:1 and Genesis 1:1, revealing its profound significance as God's eternal plan and divine blueprint for all existence.

Through a detailed analysis of the Logos, Ndlovu deepens our understanding of Jesus' divine nature and the implications of John 1:1. The book also explores the tripartite structure of human nature, mirroring the divine Trinity, and the transformative power of faith in Jesus Christ.

Ndlovu reminds us that while we're created in God's image, our essence remains distinct from His. He emphasizes the importance of embracing the mysteries of the divine with humility and awe, nurturing our spiritual heart through disciplines like meditation and prayer, and hiding God's Word in our hearts to maintain a vibrant connection with Him.

Ultimately, this book invites readers to reflect on their relationship with God and their identity as empowered sons of God, living a life that honors their Heavenly Father.

CHAPTER one
Hiding God's Word in Our Hearts: A Path to Wisdom, Guidance, and Strength

The Bible's complexity and depth are fascinating, as a single verse can warrant a comprehensive, hundred-page explanation, while an entire chapter might be succinctly summarized in just one verse. This paradox highlights the scriptures' unique nature and intentional design. The Bible was written to be universally understood and relatable, transcending time, geography, culture, and socio-economic status.

Its authors, inspired by God, employed a range of literary genres, from poetry to prophecy, to convey timeless truths and principles. This diversity allows for varying levels of interpretation and application, making the Bible accessible to people from all walks of life.

The scriptures' multifaceted nature enables readers to glean insights and understanding in different ways, depending on their individual perspectives and needs. A single verse might contain layers of meaning, requiring extensive exposition, while a chapter's central message might be distilled into a concise, impactful statement.

This adaptability ensures the Bible's relevance across centuries, cultures, and contexts, speaking to fundamental human experiences and questions. Its capacity to be both simple and profound, straightforward and complex, is a testament to its enduring power and wisdom.

We're going to explore a powerful verse in Psalm 119:11, which says, "Your word have I hidden in my heart, that I might not sin against you." Let's break it down and see how we can apply it to our lives.

The psalmist is saying that he has hidden God's Word in his heart. But what does it mean to "hide" something in your heart? It means to treasure it, to store it safely, and to keep it close. Think of your heart like a treasure chest where you keep your most precious possessions. When we hide God's Word in our hearts, we're choosing to make it a part of us. We're allowing it to shape our thoughts, our feelings, and our actions. We're saying, "God, I want Your Word to be the guiding force in my life."

But why does the psalmist want to hide God's Word in his heart? He says it's so he might not sin against God. Sin is anything that separates us from God, anything that goes against His will. When we know God's Word, we know what He expects from us. We know how to live in a way that pleases Him.

So, how can we hide God's Word in our hearts like the psalmist? In general terms, the best way to get to know God's Word is to read the Bible regularly, choose verses that speak to us, and memorize them, take time to think about what we've read and how we can apply it to our lives, and share what we've learned to help us remember it better.

Remember, hiding God's Word in our hearts is a choice we make every day. It's a choice to prioritize our relationship with Him, to seek His guidance, and to live in a way that honors Him.

Let's make a commitment to hide God's Word in our hearts, just like the psalmist. Let's choose to treasure it, to store it safely, and to keep it close. As we do, we'll find that we're better equipped to live the life God wants us to live – a life that's pleasing to Him and fulfilling for us.

Purposely, let's break down this verse slowly and deliberately, exploring its syntax, significance, and setting to uncover its full significance.

The authorship of Psalm 119 remains a topic of debate among scholars, with traditional attribution to King David. However, many experts argue that the Psalm's unique style, structure, and theological themes suggest a later composition, possibly during the post-exilic period (586-539 BCE). The Psalm's acrostic structure, where each section begins with a successive letter of the Hebrew alphabet, is more characteristic of later Hebrew poetry.

While Davidic authorship is possible, the majority of scholars consider it unlikely due to the Psalm's distinct language, themes, and theological concepts, which diverge from David's other Psalms. The true author remains anonymous, as the Psalm itself does not provide explicit attribution.

Despite the uncertainty surrounding its authorship, Psalm 119 continues to inspire and guide readers with its timeless themes of devotion, obedience, and love for God's law. One verse, in particular, resonates with the spirit of David, the man after God's own heart: "I have hidden Your word in my heart, so that I might not sin against You" (Psalm 119:11).

This verse echoes David's heartfelt desire to please God and live according to His will, as expressed in Psalms like 51 and 139. The sentiment also aligns with David's life story, marked by his passion for God's law and his desire to follow it, despite his flaws and mistakes.

While the authorship of Psalm 119 may remain uncertain, the Psalm's message and themes continue to speak to readers across centuries, offering guidance, comfort, and inspiration. The anonymity of the author serves as a reminder that the true authority and power lie not in the writer but in the Word itself, which has the ability to transform and renew hearts.

The authorship of the New Testament book of Hebrews has been a topic of debate among scholars for centuries, with some attributing it to Paul and others arguing that the writing style and language differ significantly from Paul's other epistles. However, I believe that Paul himself wrote the book of Hebrews with his own hand, and here's why:

In Paul's other letters, such as 1 Corinthians and Galatians, he mentions using a stenographer or scribe to write down his words (1

Corinthians 16:21, Galatians 6:11). This was a common practice in ancient times, where a speaker would dictate their thoughts to a writer, who would then pen the letter in their own style. However, in these same letters, Paul takes the pen from the scribe and writes the final greetings in his own hand, indicating a personal touch and authenticity.

Given this practice, it's possible that Paul wrote the entire book of Hebrews himself, without the use of a stenographer. This would explain the unique writing style and language, which differs from his other letters. In fact, the book of Hebrews is notable for its sophisticated language, elaborate arguments, and extensive use of Old Testament quotations, which may suggest that Paul wrote it himself, without the intermediary of a scribe.

Similarly, the authorship of Psalm 119 is attributed to David, and while we can't know for certain whether he wrote it in his own hand, it's clear that the psalm reflects his personal style and language. It's possible that David used a different scribe or wrote it himself, which would explain the unique characteristics of this psalm compared to others.

And so, while the authorship of Hebrews and Psalm 119 may be debated, the evidence suggests that Paul and David may have written these texts themselves, with their own hands and styles. This highlights the importance of considering the historical context and writing practices of ancient times when interpreting Scripture.

Although the authorship of Psalm 119 is uncertain, for the purpose of this study, we'll attribute it to David, emphasizing his unique relationship with God. The phrase "after God's own heart" distinguishes David from other psalmists, highlighting his exceptional devotion. Let's explore the significance of David being described as a man "after God's own heart."

In biblical contexts, the prepositions "in" and "after" have distinct meanings. "In our image" (Genesis 1:26) signifies that God created humans with a shared nature or essence, reflecting His characteristics like reason, morality, and spirituality. This refers to the inherent qualities that make us human. On the other hand, "after our likeness" (Genesis 1:26) suggests that humans are created to resemble God in terms of dominion, authority, or representation, indicating our functional role or purpose.

When God describes David as a man "after my heart" (Acts 13:22), it means that David's desires, values, and intentions align with God's. This alignment demonstrates David's devotion, loyalty, and willingness to follow God's will. The use of "after" implies a sense of alignment, conformity, or correspondence, rather than direct equivalence. David's heart is not identical to God's, but it is aligned with God's desires and values.

So, the phrases "in our image," "after our likeness," and "after my heart" convey distinct meanings. "In our image" refers to the inherent qualities that make us human, "after our likeness" refers to our functional role or purpose, and "after my heart" describes David's alignment with God's desires and values, highlighting his exceptional devotion and loyalty.

In summary, as we continue to explore the significance of Psalm 119:11 and its application to our lives, hiding God's Word in our hearts requires that we first understand its importance and its significance.

The Bible is not just a book of rules or history; it's a guide for living a life that pleases God. It contains wisdom, encouragement, and guidance for every situation we face. By hiding God's Word in our hearts, we're choosing to make it our foundation, our compass, and our source of strength.

Reading the Bible regularly is essential to hiding God's Word in our hearts. Take time each day to read a portion of Scripture, asking God to speak to you through His Word. As we read, we'll discover verses that resonate with us, and we can commit them to memory, repeating them to ourselves throughout the day.

Reflecting on what we've read is also crucial. Take time to think about what you've read and how you can apply it to your life. Ask yourself questions like "What is God saying to me through this passage?" or "How can I apply this truth to my situation?" This reflection will help us internalize God's Word and make it a part of us.

Sharing what we've learned with others is another way to hide God's Word in our hearts. When we share our insights with others, it helps us remember and apply them. We can share with friends, family, or a small group, and ask them to hold us accountable.

Consistency is key to hiding God's Word in our hearts. Make it a daily habit to read, reflect, and share God's Word. As we do, we'll find that God's Word becomes our guiding force, shaping our thoughts, feelings, and actions.

In the next chapter, and several thereafter, we'll explore the significance of the relationship between the Word of God and its relationship with God, and how it relates to Psalm 119:11. We'll examine what is truly meant by the Word that was present from the beginning of all creation, and how hiding it in our hearts entails more than just a general understanding of it.

2 CHAPTER two
In the Beginning: Understanding the Profound Implications of Berēshîth

As Christians, we may find the New Testament more relatable and easier to understand than the Old Testament. When we come across a story or account in the New Testament, we tend to accept its counterpart in the Old Testament more readily. For instance, the concept of hiding God's Word in one's heart, as mentioned in Psalm 119:11, can be further illuminated by John 1:1-5.

To gain a deeper understanding, let's start by examining the meaning of the term 'Word' itself, or better still, let's start by examining the term 'In the beginning' used in John 1:1 and Genesis 1:1. To distinguish it as a unique concept, we may need to capitalize the first letter of 'Beginning', rendering it as 'In the Beginning'. This subtle change acknowledges 'The Beginning' as a distinct entity or name, setting it apart from a general beginning.

By capitalizing the "B" in "Beginning", we're implying that it's a proper noun or a specific title, rather than a common phrase. This nuanced distinction can help us better understand the significance and implications of this term in the context of biblical narrative.

Words are the fundamental building blocks of language, serving as the primary tools for conveying thoughts, ideas, and messages. They play a vital role in facilitating communication, enabling us to express ourselves, share knowledge, and connect with others. Without words, we would struggle to articulate our thoughts, emotions, and intentions, leading to confusion, misinterpretation, and potential misunderstandings.

Words possess a unique ability to define, describe, and clarify complex concepts, allowing us to convey nuanced ideas with precision and accuracy. They provide a shared vocabulary, enabling individuals to comprehend and interpret meaning in a common way. This shared understanding is essential for effective communication, collaboration, and relationship-building.

The power of words lies in their ability to convey specific meanings, enabling us to express ourselves and understand others. As culture, technology, and society evolve, new words emerge, and existing ones adapt. Words play a crucial role in establishing the tone, atmosphere, and setting for communication, and they can evoke emotions, ranging from joy and inspiration to empathy and understanding. Words allow us to record, share, and pass down knowledge, stories, and history, facilitating artistic expression, imagination, and innovation. Furthermore, words help establish trust, empathy, and connection with others in relationships.

And so, words are indispensable to language, serving as the foundation for communication, expression, and understanding. They define, describe, and clarify ideas, enabling us to convey complex thoughts and emotions with precision and accuracy. As the building blocks of language, words play a vital role in shaping our relationships, culture, and society.

The phrase "in the Beginning" in Genesis 1:1 and John 1:1 holds profound significance and must be understood within the context of the original languages and cultures in which they were written. In Hebrew, "in the beginning" is translated as "Berēshîth" (בְּרֵאשִׁית), while in Greek, it's rendered as "archē" (αρχή).

The Hebrew word "Berēshîth" carries a richer meaning than its English counterpart, conveying a sense of eternity past rather than a specific point in time. This understanding is rooted in the Hebrew concept of "olam" (עוֹלָם), which encompasses both the infinite past and the infinite future. In this context, "Berēshîth" points to the eternal nature of God, existing beyond the bounds of time.

Similarly, the Greek word "archē" signifies not only a beginning but also a source, origin, or foundation. This nuance highlights the idea that God is the uncaused Cause, the uncreated Creator, and the eternal Source of all existence.

Therefore, when interpreting "in the beginning" in Genesis 1:1 and John 1:1, it's essential to consider the depth and complexity of the original languages. Rather than solely focusing on a temporal starting point, we're invited to contemplate the eternal and infinite nature of God, who exists beyond the confines of time and space.

Once again, for emphasis, the phrase "in the beginning" (Berēshîth) is not merely a reference to a point in time, but rather an allusion to eternity past, encompassing the infinite and timeless realm of God. This concept is rooted in the Hebrew understanding of "olam" (עוֹלָם), which transcends human notions of chronology.

Berēshîth represents not only the period of beginnings but also the divine blueprint or plan, spanning from creation to the Second Coming of Jesus Christ, and extending into eternity. This eternal plan is the framework for God's redemptive story, unfolding throughout human history.

Significantly, Berēshîth marks the initiation of the conflict between Christ and Satan, as hinted at in the proto-gospel of Genesis 3:15. This passage contains the first announcement of the good news of salvation, foreshadowing the ultimate triumph of Christ over evil.

In this sense, Berēshîth serves as the foundation for the entire biblical narrative, encompassing God's intentional design and bringing into being the universe and humanity. This includes humanity's rebellion and the entrance of sin, which sets the stage for redemption. Thus, God's plan to restore humanity culminates in Jesus Christ's life, death, and resurrection. Additionally, it includes the plan for Christ's ultimate triumph, ushering in a new creation and eternity with God.

Berēshîth, therefore, represents the eternal and timeless realm of God's plan, encompassing all of human history and beyond, with the conflict between Christ and Satan serving as the underlying tension driving the narrative forward.

The Jewish people hold the word Berēshîth (בְּרֵאשִׁית) in high esteem, as it marks the beginning of the Book of Genesis in the Hebrew Bible (Torah). This first word of the creation narrative carries profound significance, both religiously and culturally. Berēshîth translates to "in beginning" or "in the beginning," signifying the commencement of God's creative work.

The Berēshîth parashah (Genesis 1:1–6:8) encompasses several pivotal events:

1. God's creation of the heavens, the world, and humanity (Genesis 1-2)
2. The story of Adam and Eve, including their temptation by the serpent and expulsion from the Garden of Eden (Genesis 2-3)
3. The tragic tale of Cain and Abel, where Cain becomes the first murderer (Genesis 4)
4. The genealogy of Adam and Eve's descendants (Genesis 5)

Jewish communities annually read the Berēshîth portion on the first Sabbath after Simchat Torah (usually in October) and during Simchat Torah itself. In traditional Sabbath Torah reading, Berēshîth is divided into seven readings (aliyot), with further subdivisions within each reading.

The significance of Berēshîth extends beyond the Jewish community, as the opening words of the Gospel of John ("In the beginning was the Word...") allude to the Torah's Berēshîth. This intentional reference emphasizes the continuity between the Old and New Testaments, highlighting the shared heritage and theological themes.

Furthermore, Berēshîth has been interpreted in various ways throughout Jewish history:

1. Rashi (11th-century commentator) saw Berēshîth as emphasizing God's sole creation of the world.

2. Maimonides (12th-century philosopher) viewed Berēshith as a reference to the eternal nature of God.

3. Kabbalistic tradition (medieval mysticism) interprets Berēshîth as a symbol of the infinite and the divine.

And so, Berēshîth holds a revered place in Jewish tradition, marking the beginning of the creation narrative and encompassing fundamental themes and events. Its significance extends beyond the Jewish community, influencing Christian theology and interpretation.

The Berēshîth we're focusing on is the primordial blueprint of all existence, as described in John 1:1 using the past tense. This ancient Berēshîth had already transpired by the time John penned his Gospel, unlike human beginnings, which encompass an individual's entire lifespan, culminating in death – the end of the beginning and the beginning of the end.

In contrast, the Berēshîth mentioned by John was a singular, completed event that spanned a specific era or age, during which the foundation for all creation was laid. This primal era had passed, and the plans set in motion during that time were now fully operational, unfolding according to the original design. The blueprint had been executed, and the creation was functioning as intended.

This Berēshîth represents the eternal, timeless realm of God's plan, encompassing the entirety of human history and beyond. It's the source of all existence, where the divine intent was set in motion, giving rise to the universe and its intricate workings.

John's reference to Berēshîth in the past tense underscores the idea that this foundational era had already occurred, and its consequences were now being experienced. The things created during this time – the heavens, the earth, humanity – were all functioning according to the original plan, with their purposes and destinies unfolding as intended.

In essence, the Berēshîth described by John is the divine starting point, where the blueprint for all existence was established, and the course of human history was set in motion. This ancient beginning continues to shape the present and future, a testament to the enduring power of God's creative intent.

In summary, the phrase "In the Beginning" (Berēshîth) holds profound significance, encompassing the eternal and timeless realm of God's plan. It represents the divine blueprint for all existence, spanning from creation to the Second Coming of Jesus Christ and extending into eternity. Berēshîth marks the initiation of the conflict between Christ and Satan, sets the stage for redemption, and serves as the foundation for the entire biblical narrative. This concept transcends human notions of chronology, symbolizing the infinite and divine. The significance of Berēshîth extends beyond the Jewish community, influencing Christian theology and interpretation, and emphasizing the continuity between the Old and New Testaments. Ultimately, Berēshîth represents the divine starting point, where the blueprint for all existence was established, and the course of human history was set in motion.

3 CHAPTER three
The Depth and Complexity of the Word: Unveiling the Significance of Logos in John 1:1

John 1:1 a2.
... "the Word" ,...

As previously noted, it's crucial to delve into the depth and complexity of the original languages when seeking to comprehend a word, especially when that word is the Word itself. By capitalizing the "W" in "Word", we're designating it as a proper noun or a distinct title, distinguishing it from a common phrase. This subtle distinction also sets it apart from the ordinary word, "word". This nuanced differentiation enables us to more accurately grasp the significance and implications of this term within the context of the biblical narrative, revealing the profound meaning and importance of the Word.

Now, let's explore the concept of "the Word", specifically the Logos (as distinct from Rhema). In Greek, Logos (λόγος) is derived from the verb "legein", meaning "to speak" or "to utter". It encompasses the idea of a thought or concept being expressed through language, making it the manifestation of a mental idea or plan. Logos represents the external expression of an internal thought, essentially the verbalization of a concept or idea.

In philosophical and theological contexts, Logos has been interpreted as the rational principle or reason that governs the universe. In ancient Greek philosophy, Logos was seen as the source of order and structure in the cosmos.

In Christian theology, Logos takes on a more profound significance, as it is identified with Jesus Christ, the incarnate Word of God (John 1:1-14). This understanding emphasizes the idea that Jesus is the ultimate expression of God's thoughts, plans, and purposes.

In contrast, Rhema (ῥῆμα) refers to a specific spoken word or utterance, often emphasizing the immediate and personal application of God's Word in one's life.

While there is some overlap between the two words, Logos and Rhema have distinct emphases. Logos tends to focus on the abstract concept or idea, encompassing the underlying thought, reason, or principle. It represents the mental construct, the idea itself, and the intellectual understanding. On the other hand, Rhema focuses on the concrete expression or utterance, emphasizing the spoken word, the declaration, or the proclamation. It represents the verbalization of the idea, the actual words used to convey the thought. In essence, Logos is the thought, while Rhema is the spoken word that expresses that thought. This distinction highlights the dynamic relationship between the abstract concept and its concrete expression, underscoring the importance of both in conveying meaning and understanding. By recognizing this nuance, we can gain a deeper appreciation for the richness and complexity of biblical language.

There are several other Greek words related to "word" or "speech" apart from "Logos" (λόγος) and "Rhema" (ῥῆμα). Epaggeleia (ἐπαγγελία) means "announcement" or "promise", Propheteia (προφητεία) means "prophecy" or "utterance", Didache (διδαχή) means "teaching" or "doctrine", Parresia (παρρησία) means "bold speech" or "plain speaking", Lalia (λαλιά) means "talk" or "prattle", Phone (φωνή) means "voice" or "sound", and Pheme (φήμη) means "saying" or "report". Each of these words has its own nuances and connotations, and they are used in different contexts throughout the New Testament to convey various aspects of communication, speech, and language.

Back to Logos! By understanding Logos as the expression of thought and concepts, we can appreciate the depth and richness of the biblical concept of "the Word," and its significance in revealing God's nature, plans, and purposes.

To reiterate for emphasis, the phrase "the Word" (Greek: Logos) is broadly understood to refer to Jesus Christ, as further clarified in subsequent verses within the same chapter and reinforced in other passages, such as Revelation 19:13, which explicitly identifies Jesus as "the Word of God".

In John 1:1, the term "the Word" refers specifically to "Logos", not "Rhema". While "Rhema" denotes a spoken word or utterance, emphasizing the act of speaking, "Logos" encompasses a broader meaning, conveying both the idea of reason and the spoken word. In classical Greek, Logos signifies the expression of thought, intention, or rational principle, making it a more profound and nuanced concept than Rhema.

The intricate relationship between reason and word is inseparable, as every word inherently implies a thought or idea. This symbiotic connection is rooted in the nature of language itself, where words serve as vessels for conveying thoughts, concepts, and intentions. In the context of John 1:1, the term "Logos" embodies this union, representing both the rational principle and the spoken word.

The eternality of God and thought are intimately connected, as God's existence is characterized by an eternal and infinite mind. Since God always had a thought, His existence is inextricably linked with the concept of thought. This timelessness of God's thoughts is a fundamental aspect of His nature, underscoring the idea that God's thoughts are not bound by the constraints of time.

Thought, in turn, is the vehicle of speech, enabling the expression of ideas, intentions, and concepts. This is where "the word" (Logos) comes into play, serving as the manifestation of God's thoughts. Logos represents the external expression of God's internal thoughts, making it an extension of His eternal and infinite mind.

In philosophical and theological contexts, this concept has far-reaching implications. It suggests that God's thoughts are not static or passive but dynamic and creative, giving rise to the universe and all that exists. The Logos, as the embodiment of God's thoughts, becomes the agent of creation, wisdom, and reason.

This understanding is reinforced by various biblical passages, such as Psalm 33:6, which states, "By the word of the Lord the heavens were made," and Hebrews 11:3, which affirms, "By faith we understand that the universe was created by the word of God." These verses underscore the creative power of God's thoughts, as expressed through the Logos.

And so, the inseparability of reason and word, as embodied in the Logos, reveals the profound nature of God's thoughts and their role in shaping reality. This eternal and infinite mind, characterized by an unbroken stream of thoughts, gives rise to the universe and all that exists, making the Logos an integral aspect of God's creative and redemptive work.

In other words, the Word (Logos) represented God's internal reasoning, intellect, or mental conception - the very essence of His mind. It was the embodiment of God's thoughts, wisdom, and rational principle, serving as the blueprint for creation and the expression of His divine intent.

I firmly believe that the term "Logos" in John 1:1 should have been left untranslated, as it carries a rich and complex meaning that goes beyond the English word "Word". Logos encompasses a depth of significance that is lost in translation, conveying a sense of reason, wisdom, and divine logic that is fundamental to understanding the nature of God and Jesus Christ.

Just as the name "Jesus" means Savior, but holds a profound significance that transcends its literal meaning, and "Christ" means the Anointed, but is more than just a title - Jesus Christ is a name that embodies the entirety of His mission, character, and divinity. Similarly, Logos is more than just a word; it represents the very essence of God's being, His creative power, and His self-expression.

Leaving Logos untranslated would have preserved its unique connotations and nuances, allowing readers to grasp the fullness of its meaning. By using "Word" as a translation, we risk reducing the complexity of Logos to a single, oversimplified concept.

As mentioned earlier, in ancient Greek philosophy, Logos was a central concept that represented reason, wisdom, and the principle of order in the universe. In the context of John 1:1, Logos takes on an even deeper significance, identifying Jesus Christ as the embodiment of God's wisdom, creativity, and redemptive power.

By appreciating the richness of Logos, we can gain a deeper understanding of the divine nature of Jesus Christ and the profound implications of John 1:1, which affirms that Jesus is not only the Word of God but also God Himself, eternally existing and creating.

The Apostle John uniquely utilized the title "Word" (Logos) in his writings, setting him apart from other New Testament authors. Beyond the iconic John 1:1-2, he also commenced his First Epistle with a modified version of this title, stating, "That which was from the beginning, which we have heard, which we have seen with our eyes, which we have looked upon, and our hands have handled, of the Word of life" (1 John 1:1). This deliberate choice of words reinforces John's emphasis on the centrality of Jesus Christ as the embodiment of God's Word.

John's exclusive use of the "Word" title underscores his distinct theological perspective, which highlights the inseparable connection between Jesus Christ and God's creative, redemptive, and revelatory work. By invoking the "Word of life," John reaffirms the idea that Jesus is the source of eternal life, the manifestation of God's wisdom, and the agent of salvation.

Furthermore, John's repetition of the "Word" title creates a sense of continuity between his Gospel and Epistle, underscoring the coherence of his theological vision. This intentional literary device serves to reinforce the significance of Jesus Christ as the Logos, solidifying His position as the cornerstone of John's theology.

In both John 1:1-2 and 1 John 1:1, the "Word" title assumes a deeper meaning, transcending mere linguistic expression. It represents the divine logos, the creative power, and the self-expression of God, which became incarnate in Jesus Christ. By employing this title, John masterfully conveys the profound mystery of the Incarnation, where the eternal Word of God assumes human form, ushering in a new era of redemption and revelation.

In Revelation 19:13, Jesus Christ is depicted as "clothed with a vesture dipped in blood; and his name is called The Word of God." This apocalyptic imagery evokes a profound connection between Jesus and the concept of Logos, which was deeply rooted in Jewish tradition and the Wisdom literature of the Old Testament. When John designated Jesus as "the Word of God," he likely drew upon this rich cultural and theological heritage.

In the Old Testament, the phrase "the Word of God" (Hebrew: דְּבַר יְהוָה, dabar Yahweh) frequently appeared, signifying the revelation or message of God to His prophets and people (e.g., Jeremiah 1:4, Ezekiel 1:3, Hosea 1:1). John's use of "the Word of God" may have intentionally echoed this phraseology, emphasizing Jesus as the ultimate revelation, message, or communication from God to humanity.

In essence, Jesus Christ embodied the entirety of God's written and spoken Word, as expressed in the Hebrew Bible. He was the incarnation of God's wisdom, creative power, and redemptive purpose. As the Logos, Jesus was the living, breathing manifestation of God's self-expression, making Him the ultimate source of truth, guidance, and salvation.

By identifying Jesus as "the Word of God," John underscored the continuity between the Old Testament revelation and the New Testament fulfillment. Jesus was not only the messenger but also the message itself, the embodiment of God's wisdom, love, and redemption. This christological affirmation resonates throughout the Johannine literature, solidifying Jesus' position as the central figure of God's plan of salvation.

Just as he says that no one goes to the father except by him, for he's the way, the truth and the life, and no one comes to him except the father draws them to him, so no messages bypasses him to either way. He is the message itself.

Jesus is, therefore, the expression, revelation, and communication of the Lord. He is both the incarnate and inspired Word.

The Word, Jesus Christ, has an intimate and dynamic relationship with God, characterized by active and personal communication. This mirrors the Old Testament era, where God dwelled among His people in the tabernacle, a portable tent of meeting. Within this sacred space, God spoke to His people, revealing Himself and His plans (Exodus 33:7-11, Numbers 12:5). Similarly, the Word, Emmanuel, "God with us" (Matthew 1:23), tabernacled among humanity, taking on flesh and dwelling among us (John 1:14).

In this incarnate form, Jesus Christ, the Logos, became the conduit for God's communication with humanity. Through Jesus, God speaks to us, revealing His heart, mind, and purposes. This concept is reinforced in Hebrews 1:1-2, which states that God, having spoken through prophets in the past, has now spoken to us through His Son, Jesus Christ.

The tabernacle imagery is significant, as it symbolizes God's desire for proximity and communion with His people. By dwelling among us, Jesus, the Word, facilitates a deeper understanding of God's nature, character, and intentions. Through His life, teachings, death, and resurrection, Jesus reveals the Father's love, grace, and redemption.

In essence, the Word, Jesus Christ, is the ultimate expression of God's communication with humanity, embodying the divine message, wisdom, and power. As we engage with Jesus, the Logos, we encounter the living God, who speaks to us, guides us, and transforms us through His active and personal presence.

In brief summary, the concept of Logos in John 1:1 unveils the profound significance of Jesus Christ as the embodiment of God's thoughts, plans, and purposes. As the external expression of God's internal thoughts, Logos represents the rational principle, wisdom, and creative power of God. Jesus, the incarnate Word, is the ultimate revelation, message, and communication from God to humanity, embodying the divine nature, wisdom, love, and redemption. Through His life, teachings, death, and resurrection, Jesus reveals the Father's heart, mind, and purposes, facilitating a deeper understanding of God's character and intentions. As the Word, Jesus is the source of eternal life, truth, guidance, and salvation, solidifying His position as the central figure of God's plan of salvation. By appreciating the richness and complexity of Logos, we can gain a deeper understanding of the divine nature of Jesus Christ and the profound implications of John 1:1, which affirms Jesus as the eternal, creative, and redemptive Word of God.

4 CHAPTER four
The Eternal Embrace: Unveiling the Inseparable Relationship between God and the Word

The profound statements in John 1:1b and John 1:2 reveal a deeply intimate relationship between God and the Word (Logos). These two verses form a complementary circle, where the subject of one verse becomes the object of the other, and vice versa.

John 1:1b states, "the Word was with God" (Greek: "ho logos ēn pros ton theon"), emphasizing the Word's eternal existence alongside God. Meanwhile, John 1:2 declares, "The same was in the beginning with God" (Greek: "houtos ēn en archē pros ton theon"), underscoring the Word's presence with God from the very beginning.

The Greek phrase "ho logos ēn pros ton theon" is a reciprocal expression, implying a mutual relationship between God and the Word. The preposition "pros" (πρός) indicates a face-to-face or side-by-side relationship, suggesting intimacy, proximity, and reciprocity.

By saying "The Word was with God," the phrase also implicitly means "God was with the Word." This reciprocal understanding highlights the inseparable and harmonious relationship between God and the Word, emphasizing their eternal, face-to-face communion.

Before we continue, let's explore this reciprocality. At times words have similar connotations but different meanings, and vice versa.

For example, in Genesis 2:18, "I will make him a helper" (Hebrew: עֵזֶר, ezer), refers to a companion, partner, or assistant who complements and supports the other person. In this context, the helper is someone who provides aid, comfort, and partnership, making life more manageable and enjoyable.

In Psalm 54:4, "God is my helper" (Hebrew: עֹזְרִי, ozri), emphasizes God's role as a rescuer, deliverer, or assistant in times of need. Here, the helper is someone who provides strength, protection, and salvation.

While both uses of "helper" convey the idea of assistance and support, the first context focuses on companionship and partnership, whereas the second emphasizes divine intervention and rescue.

In both cases, the word "helper" implies someone who provides valuable support, but the nuances of meaning reflect the different relationships and contexts.

Another example is the word "bless", which has different connotations in these two phrases.

"God bless you" (or "God bless you all") is a common expression that means "May God bestow His favor, protection, and goodness upon you." Here, "bless" is a verb that implies God's action of conferring benefits, grace, or divine favor upon someone.

On the other hand, "My soul, bless the Lord" (Psalm 103:1-2) is a declaration that means "My soul, praise the Lord" or "My soul, extol the Lord." In this context, "bless" (Hebrew: בָּרַךְ, barak) is a verb that means to praise, extol, or give thanks to God. It's an expression of worship, adoration, and gratitude.

In the first phrase, "bless" is a request for God's favor, whereas in the second phrase, "bless" is an expression of human praise and thanksgiving towards God.

In both cases, the word "bless" carries a sense of reverence and acknowledgment of God's sovereignty, but the direction and context of the blessing differ.

There is also a word which might have a subtle difference depending on how it has been used. For example, there is a subtle difference between "I was with her" and "She was with me," even though the word "with" is used in both sentences.

The difference lies in the perspective and emphasis.

"I was with her" emphasizes your presence and companionship with her. The focus is on your actions and experiences, while "She was with me" emphasizes her presence and companionship with you. The focus is on her actions and experiences.

THE HIDDEN WORD: EXPLORING THE SECRETS OF THE HEART

In both cases, "with" indicates accompaniment, association, or togetherness. However, the subject-verb order changes the emphasis. In "I was with her," the subject is "I," and the sentence highlights your relationship or experience with her. In "She was with me," the subject is "She," and the sentence highlights her relationship or experience with you.

While the difference is subtle, it can affect the nuance and context of the sentence.

If you say "I was with her," she could indeed say "I was with him," and both statements would be true. The fact remains that you were together, and the word "with" indicates that togetherness.

In this case, the sentences are reciprocal, meaning they describe the same situation from different perspectives. Both statements acknowledge the shared experience or companionship, and the word "with" conveys that mutual presence.

So, in essence, "I was with her" and "She was with me" are interchangeable, and both convey the same basic information – that you were together. The difference lies only in the emphasis and perspective, as I mentioned earlier.

In this context, the phrases "the Word was with God" and "God was with the Word" are reciprocal statements, describing the same eternal relationship from two complementary perspectives. Both expressions convey the same truth - that the Word (Jesus Christ) and God are inseparably united, sharing a divine presence and coexistence.

Just as "I was with her" and "She was with me" describe the same togetherness from different viewpoints, "the Word was with God" and "God was with the Word" highlight the same harmonious union between God and the Word, emphasizing their mutual companionship and eternal bond.

In this sense, the phrase "The Word was with God" conveys a sense of mutual indwelling, where God and the Word coexist, interact, and relate to each other in a dynamic, personal way. This understanding reinforces the idea of their inseparable unity and distinct personhood within the Godhead.

The use of both phrases achieves a powerful effect, like killing two birds with one stone. By employing both phrases, John achieves a dual impact, effectively conveying two crucial aspects of the God-Word relationship. He emphasizes their inseparable unity, highlighting the oneness of God and the Word, while also underscoring their distinct personhood within the Godhead.

This dual emphasis reveals their eternal, harmonious relationship, precluding any attempt to separate or differentiate God from the Word. Instead, John presents the Logos as an integral, essential aspect of God's nature, demonstrating that God and the Word are distinct yet inseparable in their workings, perfectly unified in their divine operations.

To emphasize this point further, the Greek preposition "pros" (πρός) plays a crucial role, as it conveys a sense of intimate proximity and reciprocity. Translated as "with" or "toward," "pros" signifies a face-to-face relationship between God and the Word, underscoring their mutual presence, interaction, and communion. This nuanced understanding, facilitated by the precise meaning of "pros," reinforces the inseparable unity and distinct personhood of God and the Word within the Godhead. This intimate connection is further emphasized by the use of "houtos" (οὗτος), meaning "the same," which links the two verses and underscores the unity of God and the Word.

And so, John 1:1b and John 1:2 form a complementary circle, revealing the eternal, inseparable relationship between God and the Word. They are one, yet distinct persons, united in their essence and operations from the beginning of time.

John 1:1 c.
"... the Word was God."

As the Bible narrates, God created Adam from the dust of the earth, which can be more accurately described as refined clay, given the presence of water in the creation process (Genesis 2:7). This detail highlights the intentional craftsmanship of God, shaping and molding the clay into a human form. However, despite this meticulous creation, Adam remained lifeless and motionless until God breathed the breath of life into him through his nostrils. This pivotal moment marked the transformation of Adam from a lifeless soul to a living soul, as stated in Genesis 2:7, "and man became a living soul."

This distinction is crucial, as it underscores the interdependence of the soul and life. The soul, without life, is incapable of functioning, and conversely, life without a soul cannot exist. The harmonious union of the two gives rise to a living soul, enabling the individual to function, think, and exist.

Similarly, the relationship between God and His Logos (Word) mirrors this interdependence. God without His Logos is incomplete, and the Logos without God ceases to be divine. The Logos, as the expression of God's thoughts, plans, and purposes, cannot function independently of God. Conversely, God's nature and character are perfectly revealed through His Logos, making them inseparable.

This understanding is reinforced by Jesus' statement in John 10:30, "I and the Father are one," emphasizing the unity and inseparability of God and His Logos. Furthermore, the apostle John affirms this relationship in 1 John 1:1-2, describing the Logos as the "Word of life" that was "with God" and "was God."

In summary, John 1:1b and John 1:2 reveal an intimate, inseparable relationship between God and the Word (Logos). The reciprocal phrases "the Word was with God" and "the same was in the beginning with God" emphasize their eternal, face-to-face communion, underscoring their mutual indwelling and distinct personhood within the Godhead. The use of "pros" (πρός) conveys a sense of intimate proximity and reciprocity, while "houtos" (οὗτος) links the two verses, highlighting their unity. This relationship is mirrored in the interdependence of the soul and life, where God and His Logos are inseparable, each requiring the other to function and exist in harmony. Jesus' statement "I and the Father are one" (John 10:30) and 1 John 1:1-2 affirm this divine unity, revealing God and His Logos as distinct yet inseparable in their workings, perfectly unified in their divine operations.

Unlike the human soul and life, which are interdependent but cannot function as distinct persons in unison, the Logos and the Holy Spirit can operate separately yet remain in perfect harmony with God. This is similar to how multiple computers from different branches can work independently, yet their data remains synchronized with the main server. In this analogy, God is the central mainframe, and the Logos and the Holy Spirit are like satellite computers that can perform distinct tasks while maintaining seamless connectivity with the divine core.

Just as the main computer stores and processes all data, God has complete knowledge and control over the workings of the Logos and the Holy Spirit. This triune relationship allows for diverse functions and manifestations while ensuring unity and coherence in their divine operations. The Logos, as the expression of God's thoughts and plans, can create and redeem, while the Holy Spirit can inspire and sanctify, all within the framework of God's sovereign will.

This distinction highlights the unique nature of the Godhead, where distinct persons can work in harmony, each contributing to the divine plan, yet remaining inseparable from the central essence of God. This understanding underscores the complexity and beauty of the Trinity, where unity and diversity coexist in perfect balance.

Another important aspect to consider is that Jesus Christ's sonship is not a traditional familial relationship, but rather a unique and divine one. He is not the Son of God in the classical sense of a human family with a father, mother, and child. Instead, His sonship is a spiritual and theological concept that highlights His divine nature and purposeful relationship with God the Father.

In this sense, Jesus' sonship is not based on human lineage or biological descent, but rather on His divine origin and eternal existence as the Logos, the Word of God. This understanding is reinforced by scriptures such as John 1:1-3, which describe Jesus as the eternal Word who was with God and was God, and Hebrews 13:8, which affirms that Jesus Christ is the same yesterday, today, and forever.

Therefore, when we refer to Jesus as the Son of God, we are acknowledging His divine nature, His unique relationship with God the Father, and His purposeful role in human salvation, rather than implying a traditional familial connection.

Just as we acknowledge God as our Father in heaven, without implying a familial connection to a mother, we also understand Jesus' sonship in a similar manner. God is our Father in a spiritual sense, transcending human family dynamics. Likewise, Jesus is the Son of God in a unique, divine sense, untethered to traditional notions of family relationships.

This perspective highlights the distinct nature of God's fatherhood and Jesus' sonship, emphasizing their spiritual and theological significance rather than implying human-like family connections.

The Old Testament contains several verses that, while not directly referring to Jesus as the "Son of God," hold messianic prophecies and hints at His divine nature. These prophecies are later fulfilled and explicitly stated in the New Testament. One such verse is Psalm 2:7, which states, "I will declare the decree: The Lord has said to Me, 'You are My Son, Today I have begotten You.'" This suggests that the Lord declared Jesus to be the Son of God at a specific point, implying that Jesus became the Son for a particular purpose.

Acts 13:33 corroborates this idea, echoing Psalm 2:7 with the phrase "You are My Son, this day I have begotten You." The term "this day" emphasizes the moment when God declared Jesus' sonship, rather than implying an eternal sonship. Hebrews 1:5 further explains that God had not always referred to Jesus as Son, nor had Jesus always called God Father. Instead, God declared, "I will be to Him a Father, and He shall be to Me a Son," indicating a purposeful Father-Son relationship.

Similarly, Jesus was referred to as the son of David for a specific purpose (Psalm 110:1), yet He was greater than David (Mark 12:36). This suggests that the Father-Son relationship between God and Jesus served a particular purpose, rather than being an eternal designation. The fact that the Israelites knew about the Messiah, referred to as Immanuel, rather than Jesus Christ, implies that the name Jesus Christ was only officially announced for the incarnate Son.

The phrase "the name of Jesus" and "no other name but the name of Jesus" (not "the name Jesus") highlights the significance of Jesus' name and title, rather than the name itself. Additionally, Isaiah 9:6 refers to Jesus as both the Everlasting Father and the Prince of Peace, further supporting the idea of Jesus' divine nature and purposeful sonship.

Other scriptures that support this understanding include Romans 1:3-4, John 1:1-3, and Hebrews 13:8, which emphasize Jesus' divine nature, purposeful sonship, and eternal existence as God.

Jesus Christ is God.

CHAPTER 5

The Creative Power of the Logos: Unveiling the Divine Architect of the Universe

John 1:3 declares, "All things were made by him; and without him was not any thing made that was made" (KJV). Alternatively, the verse can be translated as, "All things came into being through Him, and without Him not even one thing came into being that has come into being" (NASB). This profound statement underscores the instrumental role of the Word (Logos) in the creation process. The phrase "all things" encompasses everything that exists, from the smallest subatomic particles to the vast expanse of the universe.

In this context, the verse asserts that God created everything through the agency of the Word. The Word was not merely a passive observer but an active participant in the creative process. The phrase "without him was not any thing made" emphasizes the absolute necessity of the Word in bringing all things into existence. Nothing could come into being without His involvement, underscoring His indispensable role in creation.

The verse also implies a sense of conformity to the Word's framework. Anything that didn't align with His design or purpose was deemed unsuitable for creation and therefore was not made. Only things that harmonized with His will and plan came into existence. This understanding highlights the Word's creative power and His role as the divine architect of the universe.

This concept is reinforced by other biblical passages, such as Colossians 1:16-17, which states, "For by Him all things were created, both in the heavens and on earth, visible and invisible, whether thrones or dominions or rulers or authorities—all things have been created through Him and for Him. He is before all things, and in Him all things hold together."

The apostle Paul's statement echoes the sentiments of John 1:3, emphasizing the Word's central role in creation. The phrase "all things have been created through Him and for Him" underscores the Word's agency and purpose in bringing all things into existence.

In Hebrews 1:2-3, the author writes, "In these last days He has spoken to us by His Son, whom He appointed heir of all things, through whom also He made the world. And He is the radiance of His glory and the exact representation of His nature, and upholds all things by the word of His power."

This passage further reinforces the Word's creative power and His ongoing role in sustaining all things. The phrase "upholds all things by the word of His power" highlights His continuous involvement in maintaining the universe and everything within it.

And so, John 1:3 presents a profound truth about the Word's instrumental role in creation. The verse asserts that all things came into being through Him and that nothing could exist without His involvement. This understanding underscores the Word's creative power, His role as the divine architect, and His ongoing involvement in sustaining the universe.

As the prophet Isaiah astutely observed, the Word (Logos) served as the "plumb line" or "plumb-rule" (Isaiah 28:17) for all creation, encompassing everything spiritual, material, and in every form. A plumb line, a tool used in construction to ensure straightness and alignment, symbolizes the Word's role as the divine standard or reference point for all existence.

In this sense, the Word was the ultimate benchmark, measuring and defining the alignment of all things with God's purposes and plans. He was the reference point for everything, from the intricacies of the spiritual realm to the vast expanse of the material universe.

As the plumb-rule, the Word ensured that all creation conformed to God's design, maintaining harmony, balance, and order. He was the guarantor of truth, accuracy, and precision, upholding the integrity of the universe and everything within it.

This concept is reinforced by other biblical passages, such as Proverbs 8:27-30, which describes Wisdom (a synonym for the Word) as the divine architect, guiding and directing the creation process. Similarly, Psalm 119:137 declares, "You are righteous, O Lord, and Your law is right," highlighting the Word's role in establishing the moral and ethical standards for the universe.

In the New Testament, Jesus Christ, the incarnate Word, is described as the "cornerstone" (Ephesians 2:20) and the "foundation" (1 Corinthians 3:11) of all creation, underscoring His role as the plumb-rule and reference point for all existence.

By serving as the plumb-rule, the Word ensures that all creation aligns with God's purposes, maintaining harmony, balance, and order in the universe. This understanding underscores the Word's central role in creation, His divine authority, and His ongoing involvement in sustaining all things.

After all, as Colossians 1:16 profoundly declares, all things were created through Him and, more importantly, for Him. This subtle yet significant preposition "for" underscores the ultimate purpose and destiny of creation - to exist for His glory, pleasure, and sovereign purposes. In essence, all things were created to align with His perfect will, to conform to His divine standards, and to reflect His magnificent character.

As the plumb-line and plumb-rule, Jesus Christ, the Logos, is the ultimate reference point for all creation. Every aspect of existence must be verified by Him, measured against His perfection, and compliant with His divine nature. For He is the rightful owner, the supreme authority, and the benevolent ruler over all that exists. All things are His, created to serve His purposes, to bring Him joy, and to manifest His glory.

This perspective revolutionizes our understanding of creation, shifting the focus from our own self-centeredness to His majestic centrality. It underscores that Jesus Christ is not only the agent of creation (by Him) but also the purpose and goal of creation (for Him). Everything exists to fulfill His desires, to accomplish His plans, and to radiate His splendor. In Him, through Him, and for Him, all things hold together in perfect harmony, revealing the breathtaking beauty of His divine design.

As previously mentioned, the Logos represents the thought, idea, and spoken word of God, serving as the divine medium through which God communicates and brings creation into existence. When God declared, "Let there be light" (Genesis 1:3), He spoke from His eternal idea, thought, and reason, which is embodied in the Logos. This highlights the indispensable role of the Logos in God's creative process, as without Him, God could not have spoken things into being.

This profound mystery can be challenging to comprehend, but it can be better understood by recognizing the fundamental differences between God's nature and humanity's. While God created us in His image, after his likeness (Genesis 1:26-27), He did not create us as He is. We are distinct from God, with limitations and finite capabilities, whereas God is infinite, inaccessible, eternal, and omnipotent.

One of the most fascinating aspects of God's nature is His ability to operate in three distinct persons - the Father, the Son (Jesus Christ), and the Holy Spirit - while remaining a unified, singular entity. This is evident in Jesus' statement, "He who has seen me has seen the Father" (John 14:9), which underscores the inseparable unity between the Father and the Son.

Furthermore, Jesus' conversation with Nicodemus reveals His ability to exist in both the earthly and heavenly realms simultaneously. In John 3:13, Jesus says, "No one has ascended into heaven, except He

THE HIDDEN WORD: EXPLORING THE SECRETS OF THE HEART

Who came down from heaven, even the Son of man, Who is in heaven." This statement highlights Jesus' divine nature, which enables Him to transcend spatial boundaries and exist in multiple realms at once.

Similarly, Jesus' encounter with Nathaniel (John 1:51) illustrates His role as the bridge between heaven and earth. He describes Himself as the ladder seen by Jacob (Genesis 28:12), with His feet on earth and His head in heaven, and angels ascending and descending upon Him. This vivid imagery reinforces Jesus' ability to access and connect both the earthly and heavenly realms, demonstrating His unique role as the Logos, the divine mediator between God and creation.

In other words, the Logos is so integral to God's nature that without Him, creation itself would be impossible. The Logos is not just a tool or an attribute of God, but an essential aspect of His being. To be God, He must have the Logos, and conversely, the Logos cannot exist without God. This interdependence underscores the inseparable unity between God and the Logos, highlighting that they are distinct yet indivisible.

In this sense, the Logos is not just a means by which God creates, but an essential part of God's creative power. Without the Logos, God's thoughts, ideas, and plans would remain unexpressed, and creation would not come into being. The Logos is the divine spark that brings God's creative potential to life, making it possible for Him to speak things into existence.

This understanding emphasizes the reciprocal relationship between God and the Logos, demonstrating that they are mutually dependent and inseparable. The Logos is not just a reflection of God's glory but an integral part of His nature, essential for His creative work and self-expression.

And so, John 1:3 emphasizes the instrumental role of the Word (Logos) in creation, asserting that all things came into being through

Him and nothing could exist without His involvement. The Logos is the divine architect, plumb-rule, and reference point for all existence, ensuring harmony, balance, and order in the universe. He is the thought, idea, and spoken word of God, indispensable for creation and self-expression. The Logos is integral to God's nature, and their interdependence underscores their inseparable unity. This understanding highlights the Word's creative power, divine authority, and ongoing involvement in sustaining all things, reinforcing His central role in creation and His unique position as the divine mediator between God and creation.

To reiterate and drive home this crucial point, I must stress once more: although God created us in His image and after His likeness, our fundamental essence remains profoundly distinct from His. In other words, while we bear the imprint of God's nature and reflect His character, our underlying being is not identical to His. This distinction is vital to grasp, lest we confuse our created nature with the uncreated essence of God Himself. Unlike the human soul and life, which are interconnected yet cannot function as separate entities in harmony, the Logos and the Holy Spirit possess the unique ability to operate independently while maintaining perfect unity with God. This divine capacity allows Them to be omnipresent, existing in all places simultaneously, while still dwelling in heaven, as exemplified by Jesus' statement in John 3:13 (AV), "And no man hath ascended up to heaven, but he that came down from heaven, even the Son of Man which is in heaven."

This remarkable attribute underscores the transcendent nature of God, who can exist beyond the bounds of space and time, while still being intimately present in all aspects of creation. The Logos and the Holy Spirit, as extensions of God's essence, share in this extraordinary ability, enabling Them to work in harmony with God while executing distinct roles in the divine plan.

6 CHAPTER six
The Source of Life and Light: Exploring the Dual Nature of Jesus Christ

IJohn 1:4 states that in Jesus Christ, who is the Word (John 1:1), was life, and this life was the light of humanity.

The life referred to in this verse is not just mere existence or biological life, but the source of all life, spiritual and eternal. This life is the essence of God's nature, which is characterized by love, light, and truth.

The phrase "In Him was life" signifies that Jesus is the embodiment of life, the sustainer of all creation, and the source of all spiritual vitality. The use of the past tense "was" emphasizes that this life has always existed in Him, from eternity past. However, the life in Him is not static; it is ongoing and continues to be present in Him.

The verse goes on to say, "and the life was the light of men." This life in Jesus is not only the source of spiritual vitality but also the illumination that shines in the darkness, guiding humanity towards truth, wisdom, and salvation. The "light of men" represents the revelation of God's love, wisdom, and redemption, which is made possible through Jesus Christ.

In essence, John 1:4 highlights the dual aspects of Jesus' nature: He is both the source of life and the embodiment of light. This life and light are not limited to His earthly ministry but are eternal and continue to shine brightly, offering hope, guidance, and salvation to all humanity.

Now, let's take this scripture slowly. There are three Greek words the bible uses, meaning "Life": Let's break down the three Greek words used in the Bible to describe different aspects of "Life".

The word "Zoe" refers to the uncreated, eternal life of God, which is spiritual and divine. It's the life that exists beyond physical boundaries and is often associated with salvation and eternal fellowship with God. Zoe is the life that Jesus came to offer humanity, as stated in John 1:4, "In Him was life, and that life was the light of men."

The word "Psuche" describes the psychological or soul life, encompassing our thoughts, emotions, and personality. It's the essence of who we are as individuals, including our intellect, feelings, and will. Psuche is the life that makes us human, and it's often translated as "soul" or "mind" in the Bible.

The word "Bios" refers to biological life, encompassing our physical existence and the sustenance that maintains it. Bios is the life that begins at birth and ends at death, and it's often translated as "life" or "living" in the Bible. It's the life that we experience in our bodies, with all its needs and desires.

Understanding these three Greek words helps us appreciate the richness and depth of the Bible's teachings on life. While Zoe represents eternal life with God, Psuche represents our inner life and personality, and Bios represents our physical existence. By recognizing these distinctions, we can gain a deeper understanding of the fullness of life that God offers us.

Let's delve into the fascinating story of the creation of humanity. According to the biblical account, God formed the first human, Adam, from the dust of the earth, or refined clay (Genesis 2:7). This earthy material was shaped and molded into a lifeless form, devoid of vitality. At this point, Adam was merely a motionless soul, lacking the essence of life.

Then, in a remarkable moment, God breathed the breath of life (neshamah) into Adam's nostrils, and something extraordinary happened. The lifeless body was infused with the divine spark, and Adam became a living soul, a nephesh (Genesis 2:7). This breath of life contained the psuche (the psychological or soul life) and the bios (biological life), animating Adam's body and making him a living, thinking, and feeling being.

In essence, the breath of life was the catalyst that transformed Adam from an inanimate object to a vibrant, living soul. This divine breath imparted the gift of life, encompassing both the psuche (intellect, emotions, and personality) and the bios (physical existence and sustenance). With this breath, Adam became a unique creation, possessing a body, soul, and spirit, setting him apart from the rest of creation.

This biblical account highlights the significance of the breath of life, emphasizing the divine origin of human existence. It underscores the intricate relationship between the physical and spiritual aspects of human nature, demonstrating that our lives are a harmonious blend of body, soul, and spirit.

The life we're referring to is Zoe, a Greek concept that signifies eternal life, spiritual life, or life in its fullest sense. This is the life that Jesus Christ came to offer humanity in abundance, as stated in John 10:10, "I have come that they may have life, and have it to the full." Zoe is distinct from Bios, which refers to biological life or physical existence. While Bios is limited to our earthly existence, Zoe transcends mortality and offers a deeper, more profound experience of life.

Interestingly, Psuche, another Greek term for life, occupies a middle ground between Bios and Zoe. Psuche refers to the soul or the seat of emotions, thoughts, and personality. Like Zoe, Psuche can exist beyond physical death, but it is not necessarily equivalent to eternal life. Zoe, on the other hand, represents a life that is fully alive, vibrant, and connected to God.

In essence, Jesus' promise of abundant life in John 10:10 speaks to the transformative power of Zoe, which offers a richness and fullness that goes beyond mere existence (Bios) or even the survival of the soul (Psuche). Zoe is the life that Jesus came to give us, a life that is characterized by joy, purpose, and a deep connection to our Creator.

Although it is popularly believed that Psuche means the soul, in the biblical context, Psuche (ψυχή) is often understood as the life or animating principle of the soul, rather than the soul itself. In Genesis 2:7, it is written, "and the man became a living soul" (KJV). The Hebrew word translated as "soul" is nephesh, which carries a similar meaning to Psuche. In this context, nephesh/Psuche refers to the life or vitality that animates the body, making a person a living being; hence, "man became" a living soul. This may imply that, before receiving the breath of life, Psuche, and Bios, man was a lifeless soul. Thus, in this sense, Psuche can be seen as the life or essence that makes a person alive, rather than the soul as a separate entity. This understanding aligns with the biblical view of humanity as a holistic entity, where the body, soul, and spirit are interconnected. In the New Testament, Psuche is often used to describe the life or existence of a person, as in Matthew 10:28, where Jesus says, "Do not fear those who kill the body but cannot kill the soul" (Psuche). Here, Psuche refers to the life or existence that transcends physical death.

In ancient Greek philosophy, "ζωή" (zōē) referred to the essence of life or the vital energy that gives living beings life. In Christian theology, it signifies eternal or spiritual life. In modern Greek, "ζωή" still means "life" in the sense of one's existence or lifetime. For instance, "Η ζωή μου είναι ωραία" means "My life is beautiful," and "Ζωή σε εμάς!" translates to "Cheers to life!" However, in the context of John 1:4, "ζωή" specifically refers to eternal or spiritual life, as understood in Christian theology.

On a profound note, the biblical concept of Psuche, Bios, and Zoe represents the tripartite composition of a complete person, reflecting the image and likeness of God. This mirrors the divine Trinity, where God exists as one essence in three distinct persons - Father, Son, and Holy Spirit. Similarly, humans are created with three interconnected aspects: Psuche, the Greek term for the soul or life force, representing our emotional, intellectual, and volitional capacities; Bios, the Greek word for life, signifying our physical existence, vitality, and earthly experiences; and Zoe, the Greek term for eternal life, symbolizing our spiritual rebirth and union with God, available only through faith in Jesus Christ.

The Bible reveals that God created humanity in His own image and likeness, implying a triune nature. This is reinforced by Jesus' statement, "No one has ascended to heaven but He who came down from heaven, that is, the Son of Man who is in heaven." This verse highlights Jesus' simultaneous presence on earth and in heaven, demonstrating the inseparability of the divine persons.

Similarly, humans are created with two aspects from birth, while the third is added upon spiritual rebirth through faith in Jesus Christ. This tripartite nature is echoed in the separation that occurs at death, where Bios returns to dust, Psuche returns to God who gave it, and Zoe, the eternal life, remains with God, available only to those born again.

While this understanding is rooted in biblical truth, it's essential to approach it with humility and recognition of the mysteries of God's nature and human existence. Nevertheless, this framework provides a profound insight into the intricate and wonderful design of humanity, created in the image and likeness of our triune God.

God is wonderful, inaccessible, all-wise, omni-everything. Who can understand God? His wisdom cannot be comprehended. His ways are

THE HIDDEN WORD: EXPLORING THE SECRETS OF THE HEART

unfathomable, and His thoughts are far beyond human grasp. As the apostle Paul wrote, "Oh, the depth of the riches both of the wisdom and knowledge of God! How unsearchable are His judgments and His ways past finding out!" (Romans 11:33). God's majesty is awe-inspiring, and His power is overwhelming. He is the Creator of the universe, the Sustainer of all life, and the Ruler of eternity.

Who can comprehend the mind of God? (Isaiah 40:28). His wisdom is infinite, and His understanding is boundless. He sees the end from the beginning, and His knowledge is perfect. As the psalmist exclaimed, "Great is the Lord and greatly to be praised in the city of our God, in His holy mountain" (Psalm 48:1).

Despite His inaccessibility, God has chosen to reveal Himself to us through His Word, His Son, and His Spirit. He has condescended to our level, speaking to us in a language we can understand. Yet, even as we seek to know Him, we must acknowledge the limitations of our finite minds. We can only glimpse the fringes of His majesty, and our understanding will always be incomplete.

Still, we are drawn to His wonder, like moths to a flame. We are captivated by His beauty, and our souls yearn for His presence. For in His presence, we find joy, peace, and fulfillment. As the psalmist sang, "In Your presence is fullness of joy; at Your right hand are pleasures forevermore" (Psalm 16:11).

7 CHAPTER seven
The Life and Light of Men: Understanding the Transformative Power of Christ

John 1:4 b

"... the life was the light of men."

In Him lies the essence of life, and this life transforms into the radiant light that illuminates humanity, encompassing both His devoted followers and the world at large.

However, it is only those who embrace Him who receive the gift of life, and upon receiving it, this very life within them metamorphoses into a beacon of light for the world.

Just as Christ's existence served as a revelatory catalyst, awakening humanity to God's intended perspective, so too must my life mirror this paradigm. For in the Logos – the divine Word – lies the source of life, and this life is the luminescent force that illuminates the path for humanity, guiding us toward the truth and wisdom intended by God.

In this context, Logos refers to the eternal, divine Word that became incarnate in Jesus Christ, as described in the Gospel of John (John 1:1-14). This passage emphasizes the transformative power of accepting Christ, which enables individuals to become conduits of divine light, spreading hope, wisdom, and understanding to a world in need of spiritual enlightenment.

John 1:4

" In him was life; and the life was the light of men."

We can write is as, "In him was zoe; and the zoe was the light of men."

Remember John 17:17, where Jesus says, 'Sanctify them in the truth; your word is truth.' This verse highlights the significance of God's Word as the ultimate truth. It's essential to note that the Bible doesn't say 'your word is true,' but rather 'your word is truth.' This subtle distinction is crucial, as 'to be true' and 'to be truth' have different meanings.

To be true means to be accurate or factual, whereas to be truth means to be the very essence and embodiment of truth itself. In other words, God's Word is not just a collection of true statements, but it is the personification of truth. It is the ultimate standard and source of all truth.

In this context, Jesus is praying to the Father, asking Him to sanctify believers in the truth of His Word. This implies that God's Word has the power to transform and set us apart, making us holy.

Furthermore, this verse underscores the importance of understanding that everything about God is true; there is no deceit or falsehood found in Him. However, John 17:17 takes it a step further by affirming that His Word is not just true, but it is truth itself – the very essence of His being.

This profound truth has far-reaching implications for our lives, as it emphasizes the importance of immersing ourselves in God's Word and allowing it to shape our thoughts, beliefs, and actions. By doing so, we can experience the transformative power of His truth and become more like Him.

In John 1:4, it is written, "In Him was life, and the life was the light of men." This verse reveals a profound truth about Jesus Christ, the Word of God. The "life" referred to here is not just physical existence but the divine, eternal life that Jesus embodies. This life is the source of spiritual illumination, guiding humanity out of darkness and into the truth.

As Jesus declares in John 14:6, "I am the way, the truth, and the life." He is the embodiment of truth, the path to salvation, and the source of eternal life. This life, also known as "Zoe" in Greek, is not just a gift but a transformative power that abundant life (John 10:10).

When Jesus gives this Zoe to humanity, believers become partakers of His divine nature and are empowered to reflect His light to the world. As Jesus says in John 8:12, "I am the light of the world. Whoever follows me will never walk in darkness, but will have the light of life."

Similarly, in Matthew 5:14, He teaches, "You are the light of the world. A town built on a hill cannot be hidden."

Through faith in Jesus Christ, believers become beacons of hope, shining God's light in a world filled with darkness. This light is not just a passive reflection but an active manifestation of God's love, truth, and grace. As followers of Christ, we are called to radiate this light, illuminating the path for others to follow, and pointing them to the source of eternal life – Jesus, the Truth, and the Life.

When John declares, "In Him was life, and the life was the light of men" (John 1:4), he reveals a profound truth about the transformative power of Zoe, the divine life embodied in Jesus Christ. This life is not only the source of spiritual illumination but also the catalyst for spreading God's light to humanity.

The Zoe, or eternal life, shines brightly, dispelling darkness and guiding men toward truth and salvation. Just as a prism or broken glass fragments refract light, dispersing it into various angles and spaces, believers who receive this life become instruments, reflecting and transmitting God's light to the world.

In essence, John's statement suggests that the Zoe illuminates men's understanding, revealing spiritual truth and wisdom, and empowers men to become beacons of hope, shining God's light in a dark world. This life also equips men to reflect and transmit the light, using their unique experiences and perspectives to spread the Gospel.

This concept is reinforced by Jesus' teachings, where He says, "You are the light of the world... Let your light shine before others, that they may see your good deeds and glorify your Father in heaven" (Matthew 5:14-16). He also says, "I am the light of the world. Whoever follows me will never walk in darkness, but will have the light of life" (John 8:12). As followers of Christ, we are called to embrace this Zoe, allowing it to transform us into radiant vessels, refracting God's light to a world in need of hope, guidance, and salvation. By doing so, we

THE HIDDEN WORD: EXPLORING THE SECRETS OF THE HEART

become part of a magnificent display of divine light, shining brightly for all to see.

The light emanating from celestial bodies like the solar system has captivated human imagination, leaving a profound impact on our collective consciousness. This ethereal glow has woven a rich tapestry of symbolism and wonder, transcending cultural and religious boundaries. Across the globe, light is revered as a potent symbol of knowledge, truth, and awareness, illuminating the path to understanding and enlightenment.

In various spiritual traditions, light is a recurring motif, often manifesting as a divine presence that guides seekers on their journey. Ceremonial practices and rituals frequently incorporate light as a representation of the sacred, underscoring its significance in human experience. Fables and teachings from diverse cultures feature lost souls finding their way through the guidance of light, which serves as a beacon, dispelling darkness and pointing toward clarity and righteousness.

The symbolism of light extends to its role in unveiling wisdom, dispelling ignorance, and revealing truth. It is the compass that navigates us through life's complexities, leading us toward spiritual understanding and enlightenment. In religious art, light is often depicted as a divine presence, a subtle yet powerful hint at the cosmic forces that shape our existence.

Beyond its spiritual connotations, light has a profound impact on our emotional and psychological well-being. It banishes gloom, igniting cheerfulness and shared happiness, as a single candle can spark countless others, creating a ripple effect of hope and positivity. Light offers solace, serving as a beacon at the end of the tunnel, reassuring us that truth and wisdom are within reach. Ultimately, light symbolizes the triumph of knowledge over darkness, illuminating our path toward a brighter future.

While the literal and symbolic definitions of light presented here are accurate, they only scratch the surface of the truth. In a literal sense, not all light emanates from the sun. Electric lamps, candles, fire flames, and even bioluminescent organisms like fireflies generate light independently of the ssun Moreover, from a biblical perspective, the sun is merely a reflector of light, not the source itself. According to the Book of Genesis, the solar system was created on the fourth day of creation, three days after light was first introduced. This means that for 72 hours, light existed without the presence of celestial bodies.

This primordial light is the focus of our discussion, the firstborn of creation. As described in the Gospel of John, "In the Word was life, and the life was the light of man" (John 1:4). This verse highlights the significance of light as a symbol of life, wisdom, and divine ppresence In this context, light represents the essence of creation, preceding the physical sources we know today. It's a profound reminder of the mysteries and wonders that lie beyond our everyday understanding of light.

In summary, John 1:4 reveals that Jesus Christ is the embodiment of life and light, illuminating humanity's path to truth and wisdom. The divine life, or "Zoe," transforms believers into beacons of hope, shining God's light in a dark world. This light symbolizes knowledge, truth, and awareness, guiding seekers on their spiritual journey. Embracing this life allows us to become radiant vessels, refracting God's light to a world in need of hope, guidance, and salvation. The symbolism of light extends beyond its literal meaning, representing the triumph of knowledge over darkness and illuminating our path toward a brighter future. Ultimately, the primordial light described in the Bible is the source of all life and wisdom, preceding physical sources and reminding us of the mysteries and wonders that lie beyond our everyday understanding.

When Jesus Christ declares, "I am the life, the way, and the truth" (John 14:6) and "I am the light of the world" (John 8:12), he is making profound statements about his nature and role. While his assertion of being the light of the world could be interpreted literally, as if he is the physical source of light, it's more likely that he is using metaphorical language to convey a deeper spiritual truth.

In this context, Jesus is likely saying that he is the source of spiritual illumination, guidance, and understanding. He is the one who sheds light on the path to salvation, truth, and eternal life. His statement is an invitation to follow him, to trust in his teachings, and to find direction and purpose in life through his guidance.

By claiming to be the light of the world, Jesus is asserting his divine authority and his role as the revealer of God's truth. He is the one who helps people see beyond the darkness of sin, ignorance, and uncertainty, and find their way to a deeper understanding of themselves and their place in the world.

Ultimately, while we can't know the exact nuances of Jesus' statements with absolute certainty, his declarations about being the life, the way, the truth, and the light of the world have been a source of inspiration, comfort, and guidance for countless people throughout history. We also can't rule out the possibility that he is the source of literal light, as the true nature of light itself remains uncertain and unknown to us.

And so, Jesus Christ is the embodiment of life and light, illuminating humanity's path to truth and wisdom. He is the source of spiritual illumination, guidance, and understanding, and his teachings and presence have the power to transform believers into beacons of hope, shining God's light in a dark world. Through faith in Jesus, we can experience the transformative power of his truth and become more like him, radiating light and hope to a world in need of spiritual enlightenment.

8 CHAPTER eight
The Inseparable Light: Christ and His Church Shining in DDarkness

In John 1:5a, we find a profound truth: "And the light shines in darkness; ..." This verse reveals the extraordinary nature of light, specifically the Light that is Christ, the Word and Life. After bringing light to humanity, this radiant Light continues to shine in the midst of darkness. The present continuous tense of "shines" emphasizes the ongoing, unceasing illumination.

In this context, light symbolizes truth, wisdom, and spiritual enlightenment, while darkness represents ignorance, confusion, and separation from God. The Light, embodied in Christ, persistently shines in the darkness, offering guidance and redemption. However, the darkness, lacking the capacity for understanding, fails to recognize or respond to the Light's presence.

This verse underscores the profound contrast between light and darkness, emphasizing the redemptive power of Christ, the Light that shines in the darkness, yet remains uncomprehended by it. Through this imagery, we are reminded of the boundless grace and illumination offered by Christ, even in the midst of spiritual darkness and ignorance. (We will discuss the incapability of darkness to comprehend light in the next chapter.)

Christ is the supreme Head of the Church, and the Church is His Body (Ephesians 5:23, Colossians 1:18). This intimate relationship is mutually dependent, as a head is incomplete without a body, and a body cannot function without a head. This unity is further emphasized in Colossians 1:18, where Christ is described as the "head of the body, the church." This inseparable bond makes Christ and the Church one Worker, laboring together in harmony.

As the Head, Christ is the Light of the world (John 8:12), illuminating the path to salvation and guiding humanity through spiritual darkness. Consequently, as the Body of Christ, the Church is also called to be the light of the world (Matthew 5:14). This shared identity as light-bearers underscores the Church's role in reflecting Christ's radiance, spreading His teachings, and demonstrating His love to the world.

In this sacred union, Christ, the Head, empowers the Church, His Body, to continue His mission and ministry. As the Church follows Christ's example and abides in His teachings, it becomes a beacon of hope, shining God's light in a world filled with darkness. This unity and shared purpose ensure that the Church remains an extension of Christ's presence, working together with Him to bring redemption, hope, and light to all.

The Church advances against the forces of darkness, but it cannot progress without its Head, who is Christ. For it is Christ who shines brightly in the darkness, illuminating the path forward. Yet, Christ's radiant presence is not isolated; He is inextricably linked with His body, the Church. Together, Christ and His Church form the "Inseparable-Light" that pierces through the darkness, dispelling shadows and bringing hope to a world in need. This symbiotic union enables the Church to reflect Christ's light, amplifying its impact and ensuring that His redemptive work continues unabated. As the Church moves forward, it does so with Christ at its helm, their bond an unwavering beacon of light in the darkness.

For emphasis, I come again! Jesus Christ, the Light of the world, shines brightly in the darkness, offering hope and redemption to all. As the Head of the Church, He is inextricably linked with His body, forming the "Inseparable-Light" that pierces through darkness. This union enables the Church to reflect Christ's light, amplifying its impact and ensuring His redemptive work continues. Through His sacrifice, Christ restored paradise, resurrected dead saints, and relocated paradise to the third heaven. His Church continues His mission, spreading the light of the Gospel and offering liberation to a world shrouded in darkness.

The bond between Christ and His Church is mutually dependent, with Christ empowering the Church to be the light of the world. Together, they form a beacon of hope, shining God's light in darkness. This unity underscores the Church's role in reflecting Christ's radiance, spreading His teachings, and demonstrating His love. As the Church follows Christ's example and abides in His teachings, it becomes an extension of His presence, working together with Him to bring redemption, hope, and light to all.

In this sacred union, Christ's triumphant declaration of liberation marks the inception of His universal Church, proclaiming the release of captives from darkness and the ultimate triumph over evil. Through His Church, Jesus continues to shine His light, offering hope and redemption to all generations, ensuring His victorious triumph over evil endures.

When the Word shines in darkness, it illuminates the path, much like a beacon of light in the depths of the ocean, attracting sardines and other sea creatures to its radiance. Similarly, the Word of God pierces the darkness of human ignorance and sin, drawing people to its saving light. Jesus, the Chief Fisher of men, casts His net of truth and redemption, gathering a vast catch of souls.

Just as sardines instinctively swim towards the light, many people are drawn to the Word's warmth and guidance. However, some individuals ignore the call to the light, choosing to remain in the darkness of their own understanding. But for those who respond to the invitation, God transforms them into a holy nation, His chosen people, a peculiar treasure.

As 1 Peter 2:9 (KJV) declares, "But ye are a chosen generation, a royal priesthood, an holy nation, a peculiar people; that ye should shew forth the praises of him who hath called you out of darkness into his marvellous light." This verse highlights the remarkable journey of those who leave the darkness behind, embracing the light of God's Word. They become a chosen generation, set apart for a noble purpose;

a royal priesthood, authorized to minister to others; a holy nation, dedicated to God's glory; and a peculiar people, distinguished by their commitment to the light.

In this sense, the Word's illumination is not only a call to salvation but also a summons to a life of purpose and distinction. As we bask in the radiance of God's truth, we become beacons of hope, shining forth the praises of Him who has called us out of darkness into His marvelous light.

As we bask in the radiance of God's truth, we come to realize that He is the embodiment of light, and in Him, there is no hint of darkness. The apostle John declares, "God is light, and in Him is no darkness at all" (1 John 1:5). This profound statement underscores the nature of God's being, where light represents purity, truth, and holiness.

However, our walk with God is not without its challenges. We may claim to have fellowship with Him, but if we continue to walk in darkness, we deceive ourselves and fail to live out the truth. John warns, "If we say that we have fellowship with Him and walk in darkness, we lie and do not practice the truth" (1 John 1:6). Our actions must align with our confession; otherwise, we risk severing our connection with the divine.

But when we choose to walk in the light, as He is in the light, we experience the beauty of fellowship with God and with one another. John encourages, "But if we walk in the light, as He is in the light, we have fellowship with one another, and the blood of Jesus Christ His Son cleanses us from all sin" (1 John 1:7). In this harmonious relationship, we find cleansing from sin's stain, and our bond with God and others is strengthened.

As we journey through life, may we embrace the light of God's presence, allowing it to guide us, purify us, and unite us with Him and with each other. For in the light, we find the essence of God's nature, and our lives are transformed to reflect His glory.

THE HIDDEN WORD: EXPLORING THE SECRETS OF THE HEART

As we walk in the light, we must be mindful of the darkness that surrounds us. Jesus cautioned, "But if anyone walks in the night, he stumbles, because the light is not in him" (John 11:10). This verse serves as a reminder that without the light of Christ, we are prone to stumbling and falling into darkness.

However, when we abide in the light, we are empowered to navigate through life's challenges with confidence and hope. The light of Christ illuminates our path, guiding us through the darkest of times. As the psalmist wrote, "Your word is a lamp to my feet and a light to my path" (Psalm 119:105).

In this sense, the inseparable light of Christ and His Church shines brightly in the darkness, offering hope and redemption to all. As the Head of the Church, Christ empowers His body to reflect His radiance, spreading His teachings and demonstrating His love. This unity underscores the Church's role in continuing Christ's mission, bringing light to a world shrouded in darkness.

Through His sacrifice, Christ restored paradise, resurrected dead saints, and relocated paradise to the third heaven. His Church continues His mission, spreading the light of the Gospel and offering liberation to those in darkness. The bond between Christ and His Church is mutually dependent, with Christ guiding and empowering the Church to be the light of the world.

As we journey through life, may we remain steadfast in our walk with God, embracing the light of His presence. May we shine forth the praises of Him who has called us out of darkness into His marvelous light, and may our lives be a testament to the transformative power of His love.

A fundamental principle is that God never forces individuals into righteousness, unlike the forces of darkness that seek to entice people into unrighteousness. When the light of God's presence and truth enters a person's life, darkness is instantly dispelled, fleeing from the radiance of His glory. This is because darkness is not an entity that invades, but rather the absence of light. It is the default state, present from the beginning, before the creation of light.

In this sense, believers must cherish and guard the light of God's truth, for it is the very essence of their spiritual life. When light departs, darkness quickly fills the vacuum, not because it is an active force, but because it is the natural state of absence. In reality, darkness doesn't "come" or "arrive"; it simply remains, waiting to reassert itself when the light is withdrawn.

This understanding underscores the importance of cultivating a deep and abiding relationship with God, founded on His Word and fueled by His Spirit. As believers, we must be vigilant in our pursuit of righteousness, recognizing that the departure of light creates an opportunity for darkness to reassert its presence.

The Bible reminds us that "God is light, and in Him is no darkness at all" (1 John 1:5). As we walk in His light, we are called to reflect His radiance, dispelling the darkness around us. By embracing the light of God's truth and guarding it jealously, we can ensure that darkness remains suppressed, and the presence of God remains vibrant in our lives.

In essence, the light of God's truth is the antidote to darkness, and believers must prioritize its presence in their lives. By doing so, we can experience the transformative power of God's light, and our lives will become beacons of hope in a world filled with darkness.

Furthermore, as the Word shines in darkness, the Word of Life, Jesus Christ, who is the light of man (John 1:4), illuminates the path for humanity. He is the Zoe, the divine life that radiates eternal light, dispelling the darkness of sin and ignorance. As the Light of the world (John 8:12), Jesus imparts His light to believers, empowering them to become beacons of hope in a world shrouded in darkness.

The apostle Paul wrote, "For God, who said, 'Let light shine out of darkness,' made his light shine in our hearts to give us the light of the knowledge of God's glory displayed in the face of Christ" (2

Corinthians 4:6). This divine light is not just a fleeting experience but a continuous radiance that guides us on our spiritual journey.

David's desire to hide God's Word in his heart was motivated by his desire to avoid sinning against God (Psalm 119:11). Similarly, as we treasure the Word of Life in our hearts, we are empowered to walk in the light, avoiding the snares of sin and darkness.

Jesus taught, "You are the light of the world. A town built on a hill cannot be hidden" (Matthew 5:14). As we allow His light to shine in us, we become reflections of His glory, illuminating the world around us.

By hiding the Word of Life in our hearts, we ensure a continuous radiance, a perpetual glow that guides us through life's challenges. As we abide in His light, we are transformed into beacons of hope, shining forth the praises of Him who has called us out of darkness into His marvelous light (1 Peter 2:9).

The city built atop the hill cannot be hidden, for it is a beacon of light, shining brightly for all to see (Matthew 5:14). This city represents the collective body of believers, each one a house with its own light, radiating the glory of God. Just as individual lights come together to form a dazzling display of brilliance, the combined efforts of believers create a radiant city that cannot be ignored.

Jesus taught, "You are the light of the world... Let your light shine before others, that they may see your good deeds and glorify your Father in heaven" (Matthew 5:14, 16). As we hide the Word of God in our hearts, we become individual lights, shining where we are, and together, we form an unstoppable force, illuminating the world with the combined strengths of our lights.

The apostle Paul wrote, "For just as each of us has one body with many members, and these members do not all have the same function, so in Christ we, though many, form one body, and each member belongs to all the others" (Romans 12:4-5). This unity is the key to our collective radiance, as we come together, each contributing our unique light, to form a dazzling display of God's glory.

Let us not ignore the power of unity, each of us hiding the Word of God in our hearts, shining our light for all to see. As we do, we will become an unstoppable force, a city built atop a hill, shining so brightly that it cannot be hidden. We will be the light of the world, reflecting the glory of God, and drawing all people to Him.

9 CHAPTER nine
The Incomprehensible Light: How Darkness Fails to Understand God's Plan

IJohn 1:5b
"... the darkness comprehended it not."

When Jesus Christ founded His universal Church, He marked its inception with a triumphant declaration of liberation, proclaiming the release of captives from the depths of Hades (Luke 4:18, Isaiah 61:1-2). As He ascended on high, from the lower parts of the earth, He led a procession of captives, binding the powers of darkness and shattering the gates of Hades (Ephesians 4:8-10, Psalm 68:18). This majestic procession was accompanied by the resurrected saints, who were seen entering Jerusalem alongside Him, testifying to the victory of life over death (Matthew 27:52-53).

This glorious event fulfilled Jesus' earlier prophecy that the "gates of Hades" – the forces of darkness and evil – would not prevail against the radiant light of His presence and the Church (Matthew 16:18). The gates of Hades, once thought impenetrable, were now breached, and the light of redemption shone brightly, illuminating the path to salvation.

In this momentous occasion, Jesus demonstrated His authority over the realms of death and the underworld, proclaiming the universal Church as a beacon of hope and liberation. As the Head of the Church, He empowered His followers to continue His mission, spreading the light of the Gospel to a world shrouded in darkness.

This event marked the ultimate triumph of Jesus over the forces of evil, as He proclaimed liberty to the captives, fulfilling the prophecy of Isaiah 61:1-2. By leading captivity captive, as stated in Ephesians 4:8-10, He demonstrated His authority over the realms of death and the underworld. Moreover, Jesus shattered the gates of Hades, as foretold in Matthew 16:18, symbolizing the destruction of the powers of darkness. Through His sacrifice, He restored paradise, as promised to the thief on the cross in Luke 23:43, and resurrected the dead saints, as witnessed in Matthew 27:52-53, thereby relocating paradise to the third heaven.

The phrase "comprehended it not" highlights the limitations of darkness. Comprehension involves processing information, connecting ideas, and gaining insight – cognitive functions that darkness, by its very nature, cannot perform. Darkness is incapable of understanding, grasping, or making sense of the complex concept of light and the profound mysteries of existence that come with it.

The event described in this passage occurred just over 2,000 years ago, when Jesus Christ, the Light of the world, was crucified on the cross at Calvary (John 3:19). Despite humanity's propensity for darkness and sin, Christ's sacrifice marked a pivotal moment in history, where the power of darkness was defeated once and for all.

The Bible describes the initial triumph of light over darkness in Genesis 1:3, where God commands, "Let there be light," and separates light from darkness. Similarly, when Christ, the embodiment of light, entered the world, He illuminated the darkness, exposing the evil that had previously shrouded humanity.

However, the darkness, personified by Satan, failed to comprehend the nature and significance of Christ's light (John 1:5). The light of Christ continues to shine in the darkness, symbolizing the ongoing struggle between good and evil.

Notably, the passage highlights that the light shines "in" darkness, not "in the" darkness. This distinction emphasizes that the light advances, dispelling darkness, while the world of darkness remains, awaiting redemption. As the light progresses, it rescues individuals from the clutches of darkness, guiding them toward righteousness.

This spiritual dynamic is ongoing, with the light of Christ continually illuminating the darkness, offering hope and salvation to those who seek it. Through His sacrifice and ongoing presence, Christ

THE HIDDEN WORD: EXPLORING THE SECRETS OF THE HEART

ensures that the light will ultimately prevail, conquering the darkness and its stronghold on humanity.

The dichotomy between light and darkness is a recurring theme throughout scripture, highlighting the fundamental incompatibility between Christ, His Church, and the forces of darkness. This antagonism is mutual, with neither party welcoming the presence of the other.

However, it's crucial to differentiate between "darkness" and "the darkness." Darkness represents the absence of light, whereas "the darkness" personifies the evil, unrighteous world, symbolized by Satan's dominion (John 12:31, 1 John 5:19).

The Bible teaches that light shines in darkness, but the darkness is incapable of comprehending or overcoming the light (John 1:5). When light advances, darkness recoils, yet the evil world system, "the darkness," remains, awaiting redemption. Christ, as the Light of the world, shines in this darkness, illuminating the path to salvation (John 8:12).

The Genesis account of creation provides a paradigm for the Church's role in this spiritual conflict. On the first day of creation, God separated light from darkness, establishing a template for the ongoing struggle between good and evil (Genesis 1:4). Initially, darkness dominated, but with the advent of light, it gave way, demonstrating the power of light to dispel darkness.

Similarly, Christ has commissioned His Church to be a beacon of light, advancing against the forces of darkness (Matthew 28:18-20, Acts 1:8). By embracing this mandate, the Church can overcome the darkness, shining the light of Christ into the world, and redeeming individuals from the clutches of evil. As the Church assumes its offensive role, darkness will continue to flee, and the light of Christ will triumph, fulfilling the promise of Revelation 21:25, where "there shall be no night there."

In God's deliberate sovereign design, the 24-hour cycle commences with evening, followed by morning, establishing a paradigm where darkness precedes light (Genesis 1:5, 8, 13, 19, 23, 31). This pattern is reflected in the Hebrew calendar, where each day begins at sunset, marking the start of a new day. This unique perspective highlights the precedence of darkness, symbolizing humanity's experience of navigating through challenges and tribulations before encountering the radiance of God's presence.

The evening, though shrouded in darkness, holds a promise of impending light. The psalmist declares, "Weeping may last through the night, but joy comes with the morning" (Psalm 30:5). This assurance underscores the hope that even amidst darkness, the light of God's presence is imminent. The morning heralds the arrival of light, banishing the shadows and illuminating the path forward. This daily cycle mirrors the spiritual journey, where believers transition from darkness to light, symbolizing their transformation from spiritual death to life in Christ (Ephesians 5:8, 1 Peter 2:9).

Notably, even in the midst of night, the light of God's creation shines through the moon and stars, foreshadowing the dawn. This celestial tapestry serves as a reminder that God's presence is always available, even when darkness seems to prevail. The light of God's Word and Life pierces the darkness, readying the heart for the fullness of His radiance. The moon and stars, created on the fourth day of creation (Genesis 1:14-19), serve as a testament to God's sovereignty and provision, even in the darkest moments.

In this paradox, we find comfort in the truth that even when surrounded by darkness, the darkness itself cannot comprehend or extinguish the light of God's presence (John 1:5). His Word, Life, and Light persist, illuminating the path and guiding us through the darkest of times. As the apostle Paul wrote, "For God, who said, 'Let light shine out of darkness,' made his light shine in our hearts" (2 Corinthians 4:6).

As believers in Christ, we are assured of a profound truth: we will not be overcome by darkness, for Christ Himself is the radiant Light that illuminates even the darkest of places. As the embodiment of light, Christ shines brightly, dispelling the shadows and guiding us through life's challenges. His presence ensures that we will never be engulfed by darkness, for He is the Light that overpowers the darkness (John 1:5).

Jesus declared, "I am the light of the world. Whoever follows me will never walk in darkness, but will have the light of life" (John 8:12). This promise is reaffirmed in John 12:46, where He says, "I have come as a light into the world, that whoever believes in me may not remain in darkness." Through faith in Christ, we are transferred from the domain of darkness to the kingdom of light (Colossians 1:13), where we bask in the warmth of His radiance.

In Christ, we possess the light of life, which enables us to navigate life's journey with hope, confidence, and wisdom. His light exposes the darkness, revealing the path forward and empowering us to overcome the obstacles that once hindered us.

Through our union with Christ, the Light of the world, we are assured of victory over darkness, and we can proclaim with conviction, "You are the light of my life; in Your light, I will see light, even in the darkest of times" (Psalm 36:9).

In a summary, the biblical narrative presents a profound dichotomy between light and darkness, symbolizing the eternal struggle between good and evil. Through the person and work of Jesus Christ, the Light of the world, darkness is defeated, and the power of light is victorious. Despite the darkness' inability to comprehend or overcome the light, the struggle persists, with the light continually advancing and rescuing individuals from the clutches of evil.

The Genesis account of creation establishes a paradigm for this spiritual conflict, where light separates from darkness, demonstrating the power of light to dispel darkness. The Church, commissioned by

Christ, assumes an offensive role, shining the light of Christ into the world and redeeming individuals from the forces of darkness.

In this spiritual dynamic, the light of God's presence, Word, and Life pierces the darkness, guiding believers through life's challenges and illuminating the path forward. As believers in Christ, we are assured of victory over darkness, possessing the light of life that enables us to navigate life's journey with hope, confidence, and wisdom.

Ultimately, the light of Christ will triumph, conquering the darkness and its stronghold on humanity, fulfilling the promise of Revelation 21:25, where "there shall be no night there."

All this was made possible by the Light that shines in darkness, and the darkness could not comprehend it. The darkness was unable to comprehend or grasp the complex concept of light and the profound mysteries of existence that came with it. Before Genesis 1:2, darkness had reigned for an unknown period. However, when light emerged, darkness was perplexed and couldn't understand what was happening. Similarly, when Christ died on the cross, Satan couldn't make sense of the shedding of Jesus' blood and its connection to humanity's salvation.

It wasn't until Christ led the universal church to victory, ascending from the paradise realm alongside Hades (as seen in the story of Lazarus and the rich man in Luke 16:19-31), that Satan realized his defeat. Jesus rose with the dead saints, and they were seen entering Jerusalem together, marking their transition to the third heaven, the new location of paradise (as described by Paul in 2 Corinthians 12:1-4, where he mentions being caught up to the third heaven, whether in the body or out of the body).

Only then did Satan comprehend the magnitude of his defeat at the hands of the Light of the world, Jesus Christ.

10 CHAPTER ten
The Word and the Heart: A Sacred Union of Divine Proportions

In Psalm 119:11, the verse states: "Thy word have I hid in mine heart, that I might not sin against thee."

In this context, the subject is David (the "I"), the object being acted upon is the Word (Thy word), and the recipient or location where the action takes place is the Heart (mine heart). The psalmist is actively hiding the Word in his heart, indicating a deliberate effort to internalize and treasure God's Word.

However, it's worth noting that, in a deeper sense, the Word and the Heart are interconnected and interdependent. The Word has the power to transform and shape the Heart, and the Heart is the vessel that receives and responds to the Word. Thus, while there is a subject-object relationship in this verse, the Word and the Heart are also intimately connected in a way that transcends a simple subject-object dichotomy.

Now that we've delved into the significance of the "Word" in relation to God, it's essential to examine the "Heart" and its role as the sacred space where the Word of God can be hidden. In the context of Psalm 119:11, the Heart represents the innermost being, the seat of emotions, thoughts, and desires. It's the center of a person's spiritual life, where faith, hope, and love reside.

In the Bible, the Heart is often associated with the emotional center, the source of emotions, feelings, and passions. It's also seen as the intellectual center, the seat of wisdom, understanding, and discernment. Furthermore, the Heart is considered the spiritual center, the dwelling place of the Holy Spirit, where God's presence is felt. Additionally, it's the moral center, the source of motivations, intentions, and actions, influencing our behavior and character.

By hiding God's Word in his Heart, David is internalizing God's truth, making it a part of his being. He's treasuring God's Word, holding it dear and precious. He's conforming his thoughts, emotions, and actions to God's will. He's cultivating a deep, personal relationship with God.

In essence, the Heart is the sacred space where the Word of God takes root, transforming and renewing us from the inside out. By hiding God's Word in our Hearts, we invite God's presence, wisdom, and guidance to shape our lives, enabling us to live according to His will and purposes.

The metaphorical heart has been a universal symbol across cultures, representing the core of human emotions, intentions, and values. It is often seen as the seat of compassion, love, and kindness, but also of malice, cruelty, and wickedness. This duality reflects the complexities of human nature, where good and evil coexist in a delicate balance.

In many ancient cultures, the heart was believed to be the dwelling place of the soul, where the divine and human realms intersected. The Egyptians, for instance, believed that the heart was the center of a person's being, where the gods communicated with mortals. Similarly, in ancient Greece, the heart was associated with the seat of the soul, where emotions, thoughts, and desires originated.

In many spiritual traditions, the heart is seen as a bridge between the physical and spiritual worlds. In Buddhism, the heart is considered the center of loving-kindness and compassion, while in Christianity, it is seen as the seat of faith and devotion. In Islamic tradition, the heart is believed to be the repository of knowledge, wisdom, and spiritual insight.

The heart is also often associated with courage, strength, and resilience. In many cultures, a person with a "heart of gold" is admired for their kindness, generosity, and selflessness. Conversely, a person with a "heart of stone" is seen as cold, unyielding, and cruel. However, the heart can also be a symbol of vulnerability and weakness. In many cultures, a person who "wears their heart on their sleeve" is seen as overly emotional, sensitive, and exposed to hurt. This vulnerability can be both a strength and a weakness, as it allows for deep connections with others but also leaves one open to pain and exploitation.

In literature and art, the heart has been a timeless symbol of human experience. From Shakespeare's "heart of darkness" to Edgar Allan Poe's "telltale heart," the metaphorical heart has been used to explore the depths of human emotion, morality, and psychology.

In modern times, the heart has become a ubiquitous symbol in popular culture, representing love, passion, and desire. From heart-shaped emojis to Valentine's Day cards, the heart has become a visual shorthand for emotions and relationships. Yet, despite its widespread use, the metaphorical heart remains a complex and multifaceted symbol, open to interpretation and reflection. It invites us to explore the depths of our own emotions, values, and motivations, and to consider the intricate balance between good and evil that exists within us all.

Ultimately, the metaphorical heart reminds us that human nature is a rich tapestry of contradictions, paradoxes, and mysteries. It encourages us to embrace our own vulnerabilities, to cultivate compassion and empathy, and to strive for wisdom, kindness, and understanding. As a symbol of both light and darkness, the heart continues to inspire, provoke, and guide us on our journey towards self-discovery and connection with others.

When we describe God's nature or actions using metaphorical language, it's possible that these descriptions are literal from God's perspective. For instance, when God says that the heart of humanity is "wicked" or "corrupt beyond healing" (Jeremiah 17:9), He may be referring to the literal heart, the physical organ, but also the spiritual center of a person. In God's view, the heart encompasses not only emotions and thoughts but also the core of a person's being, including their spiritual and moral condition.

Similarly, heavenly beings or angels may perceive our biological hearts as metaphorical or symbolic, just as we consider the center of the soul or spirit as metaphorical. This perspective highlights the complexity and multifaceted nature of human existence, comprising both physical and spiritual aspects.

This idea resonates with biblical teachings, where the heart is often described as the seat of emotions, thoughts, and spiritual life (Proverbs 4:23, Luke 6:43-45). The heart is seen as a reflection of one's true nature, influencing actions and decisions. By considering the heart in a more comprehensive and literal sense, we may gain a deeper understanding of God's perspective on humanity and the human condition.

It's essential to acknowledge that this discussion is rooted in philosophical and theological interpretation, and diverse beliefs and perspectives will inevitably vary. In this context, it's crucial to recognize that differing viewpoints represent subjective truths, not objective reality. They are informed hypotheses, educated guesses, or theoretical frameworks, but may not necessarily reflect the absolute truth. The truth, in its purest form, might transcend human comprehension, remaining elusive and beyond our reach. However, one thing is clear: when God refers to the heart, He genuinely means it. The biblical narrative consistently emphasizes the significance of the heart in God's eyes, highlighting its role as the core of human emotions, thoughts, and spiritual life (Proverbs 4:23, Luke 6:43-45, Jeremiah 17:9-10).

While we may not fully grasp the nature of the "real heart" – whether it encompasses the physical organ, the soul, or a deeper spiritual essence – God's understanding is complete. His perspective is unencumbered by human limitations, allowing Him to see the heart in its entirety.

This distinction is vital, as it acknowledges the boundaries of human knowledge while affirming God's omniscience. By recognizing the constraints of our understanding, we can approach the concept of the heart with humility, acknowledging that our perceptions are partial and provisional, while God's knowledge is absolute and definitive.

In this sense, our varied perspectives serve as approximations, attempts to grasp a reality that may ultimately surpass human comprehension. Yet, by exploring these concepts and engaging in thoughtful discussion, we can deepen our understanding and draw closer to the truth, even if it remains beyond our full grasp.

When exploring concepts we label as metaphorical, it's essential to recognize that by doing so, we acknowledge the limitations of our understanding. In essence, we confess that our knowledge about these subjects is incomplete or indirect. This is particularly significant when examining spiritual or scriptural contexts.

In the Gospel of John (1:1-5), we find a profound affirmation of the creative power of Jesus Christ, the Word of God, also referred to as the Logos. This Logos is described as the life-giving, infinite light of humanity, and the source of all creation. Notably, the text does not suggest that the Logos is a metaphor, but rather a real, divine entity that brought all things into existence.

Similarly, in Deuteronomy 29:29, Moses distinguishes between revealed and hidden knowledge, stating that "the secret things belong to the Lord our God, but the things revealed belong to us and to our children forever." Moses' statement emphasizes the distinction between the known and the unknown, without implying that the hidden things are merely metaphorical. Instead, he acknowledges the existence of mysteries that are beyond human comprehension, reserved for God's understanding alone.

By recognizing the boundaries of our knowledge and the reality of divine mysteries, we can approach scriptural and spiritual concepts with humility and awe, acknowledging the complexity and depth of God's creation.

Although our understanding is incomplete, scriptural texts can offer insights into metaphorical concepts. Some of these abstract ideas require us to connect the dots, much like the Book of Daniel prophesied that in the latter days, knowledge will increase and people will unravel some of these enigmas (Daniel 12:4). This prophecy suggests that as human knowledge and wisdom grow, we will be better equipped to decipher and comprehend complex spiritual and metaphorical truths.

Throughout history, advancements in various fields have shed light on biblical metaphors, allowing us to grasp their deeper meanings. For instance, modern psychology has helped us understand the scriptural concept of the "heart" as a symbol of our emotional and cognitive centers, rather than just a physical organ (Proverbs 4:23, Luke 6:43-45).

Similarly, scientific discoveries have illuminated biblical metaphors related to nature, such as the "waters above the firmament" in Genesis 1:7, which may be seen as an ancient description of the Earth's atmosphere. As our knowledge continues to expand, we can expect to uncover even more hidden meanings and symbolism in scriptural texts, fulfilling the prophecy of Daniel and enriching our understanding of spiritual truths.

In summary, in Psalm 119:11, David's act of hiding God's Word in his heart symbolizes the profound connection between the divine and human realms. The heart, as a metaphor, represents the intricate tapestry of human emotions, thoughts, and spiritual life, while also serving as a vessel for God's presence and guidance. Through exploring the complexities of the heart and its relationship with the Word, we gain insight into the multifaceted nature of human existence and the depths of God's perspective. By acknowledging the limitations of our understanding and embracing the mysteries of the divine, we can approach scriptural and spiritual concepts with humility and awe, ultimately deepening our connection with God and cultivating a more profound understanding of ourselves and the world around us.

11 CHAPTER eleven
The Real Heart: Unveiling the Spiritual Center of Our Being

To truly understand the concept of the heart as God intends, we must return to the foundation of creation, when God spoke the Rhema, declaring, "Let us create man in our image, after our likeness" (Genesis 1:26). This pivotal moment reveals the divine blueprint for humanity. While God and man share a commonality in having a heart, a stark contrast exists between the two: God is an eternal, immortal, and spiritual being, whereas man is a mortal, fleshly creature, formed from dust.

The distinction lies not only in their composition but also in their essence. God's heart represents the core of His divine nature, encompassing His emotions, will, and character. Conversely, humanity's heart, though fashioned after God's, is a finite, earthly representation. The biological heart, which pumps life-giving blood throughout our bodies, serves as a mere shadow or echo of the true, spiritual heart.

The spiritual heart, often wrongly referred to as the soul or inner being, is the immaterial part of humanity that resonates with God's likeness. The Bible makes a distinction between the soul and the heart, presenting them as separate entities. In Ezekiel 18:4, it states, "The soul who sins shall die," emphasizing that the soul, as a complete human entity, is accountable for its actions. The soul encompasses the entire person, including their physical, emotional, and spiritual aspects.

In contrast, the heart refers specifically to the spiritual center of a person, where emotions, thoughts, and intentions reside. While the heart is a vital part of a person, it is not the same as the soul. The soul is the person as a whole, whereas the heart is a component of that person.

To illustrate the difference, consider a person as a house. The soul is the entire house, encompassing all its rooms and aspects. The heart, on the other hand, is like the living room, where emotions, thoughts, and relationships are nurtured. Just as a house has multiple rooms, a person has multiple facets, with the heart being one essential part of the whole.

This distinction highlights the complexity of human nature, emphasizing that our spiritual, emotional, and physical aspects are interconnected yet distinct. Understanding the difference between the soul and the heart encourages us to care for and nurture our entire being, acknowledging that our spiritual heart is a vital part of our overall well-being.

Human beings were created with two interconnected yet distinct lives: the bios (physical life) and the psuche (spiritual life). Jesus Christ introduced the Zoe, a third and eternal life. When God describes David as a man "after my heart," it implies that God has a heart in both his psuche (spiritual essence) and Zoe (eternal life). Similarly, humans have a heart in their bios (physical existence), which is a reflection or shadow of the heart in their psuche (spiritual being).

When we discuss emotions, pleasures, and thoughts associated with the heart, we're referring to the psuche heart - the spiritual and emotional center of our being - rather than the physical, biological heart. In this context, the heart represents the seat of our inner life, where our feelings, desires, and thoughts reside, rather than the physical organ that pumps blood through our veins. It is this aspect of our nature that enables us to connect with God, experience emotions, and exercise free will. In essence, our spiritual heart is the seat of our deepest longings, desires, and aspirations, and it is here that we can encounter God's presence and love.

By acknowledging the dichotomy between God's infinite, spiritual heart and humanity's finite, fleshly heart, we can begin to grasp the profound significance of God's declaration. We are created in His image, with a heart that reflects His nature, yet we are also humbly reminded of our mortal limitations. This paradox invites us to explore the depths of our spiritual heart, where we can experience the divine and cultivate a deeper relationship with our Creator. Due to our finite

THE HIDDEN WORD: EXPLORING THE SECRETS OF THE HEART

understanding, we often perceive our psuche (the Greek concept of the heart or soul) and God's heart as abstract or metaphorical. However, the heart we experience is as real as the physical heart that sustains our biological body, for it performs analogous functions in our spiritual or psuche body. This parallel highlights the intricate connection between our physical and spiritual selves.

Have you ever pondered why individuals claim ownership of various aspects of themselves, such as their body, spirit, heart, soul, life, and more? Phrases like "my body," "my spirit," and "my heart" are common expressions. This possessiveness raises a profound question: Who is the entity that seems to govern and possess all these facets of our being? This enigma is challenging to solve, but it can be understood as an inherent, instinctual knowledge bestowed upon us by God, accessible only to our inner being. This inner essence, often referred to as the spirit of Man, possesses the authentic heart – the seat of our deepest emotions, intuition, and connection to the divine.

The concept of the heart as a symbol of our spiritual center is rooted in various spiritual traditions and philosophies. In ancient Greek philosophy, the heart was seen as the seat of the soul, while in many indigenous cultures, it's considered the dwelling place of the spirit. This understanding transcends the physical heart, speaking to a deeper, more profound aspect of our humanity. By acknowledging and exploring this mystery, we may gain insight into the intricate relationship between our physical and spiritual selves, and the essence that animates us – the real heart.

Remember, we're to understand Psalm 119:11, in which David declares, "Your word I have hidden in my heart, that I might not sin against You." To grasp the depth of this statement, we must understand the biblical concept of the heart. The Bible differentiates between two types of "hearts" within humans: the bios heart and the psuche heart.

The bios heart refers to the physical heart, responsible for pumping blood throughout the body. This heart is a vital organ, essential for sustaining life. In the biblical context, blood represents life itself (Leviticus 17:11, Deuteronomy 12:23). The bios heart is a remarkable example of God's design, beating around 100,000 times per day, supplying oxygen and nutrients to the body.

In contrast, the psuche heart is the spiritual heart, often translated as "mind." This heart is the seat of our thoughts, emotions, and will. It's the psuche heart that connects us to the divine, enabling us to love, worship, and obey God. Conversely, it's also susceptible to evil influences, leading us astray.

David's statement in Psalm 119:11 indicates that he has hidden God's word in his psuche heart, allowing him to resist sin and stay connected to God. This spiritual heart is the chamber where our deepest beliefs, values, and motivations reside. By storing God's word in this heart, David has chosen to prioritize his spiritual well-being, aligning his thoughts, emotions, and actions with God's truth.

In essence, David's declaration highlights the importance of internalizing God's word, allowing it to penetrate the depths of our being, and transform our lives. By hiding God's word in our psuche heart, we can cultivate a deeper relationship with Him, make wise decisions, and live a life that honors Him.

The physical heart, a vital organ in the human body, serves as a metaphor for the spiritual heart referred to in the Bible, which is the core of a person's being (psuche). Just as the biological heart pumps life-giving blood throughout the physical body, the spiritual heart is the source of spiritual life, nourishing and sustaining a person's inner being. The functions of the physical heart - pumping, circulating, and nourishing - parallel the roles of the spiritual heart, which includes pumping love, circulating faith, and nourishing hope, thereby giving life and vitality to a person's spiritual existence.

Let's explore the biological heart in detail. It is a vital organ that plays a central role in the body's functioning, earning it the title "the body's engine". It pumps blood throughout the body, supplying oxygen and nutrients to tissues and organs, and receives deoxygenated blood from the body and sends it to the lungs for oxygenation. The heart also transports nutrients from the digestive system to the body's cells and helps remove waste products from the body by circulating blood through the kidneys and liver.

The heart's continuous pumping action maintains blood flow, ensuring the body's survival. It adjusts its pumping force to maintain healthy blood pressure and increases or decreases blood flow in response to physical activity, stress, or other factors. The heart works in harmony with the lungs, digestive system, and kidneys to maintain overall health.

It is unique due to its constant activity, beating around 100,000 times per day, making it one of the hardest-working organs. Its central location facilitates blood circulation to all parts of the body, and its functioning is crucial for the body's survival, making it an indispensable organ.

In comparison to other body parts, the heart's importance cannot be overstated. It is a remarkable organ that plays a vital role in sustaining life, regulating blood flow, and adapting to changing needs. Its merit to the whole body is immeasurable, earning it a special place as the body's engine.

Just as the physical heart plays a vital role in the well-being of the body, the spiritual heart is equally crucial for the spiritual person, often referred to as the "psuche" person in biblical terms. The spiritual heart is the seat of emotions, thoughts, and character, influencing a person's relationships, decisions, and overall spiritual health.

This spiritual heart is responsible for controlling a person's emotions, such as love, joy, and compassion, as well as immaterial aspects like intuition, conscience, and faith. It is the spiritual heart that determines a person's values, motivations, and actions, ultimately shaping their spiritual destiny.

In many spiritual traditions, the state of one's spiritual heart is believed to determine their worthiness for eternal life (Zoe) or spiritual separation (hell). A heart that is pure, loving, and surrendered to a higher power is often seen as worthy of eternal life, while a heart that is filled with hatred, greed, and selfishness may be seen as destined for spiritual separation.

The concept of the spiritual heart is rooted in various religious and philosophical teachings and religions. In Christianity, Jesus taught that the heart is the source of both good and evil (Matthew 15:18-19), emphasizing the importance of spiritual heart transformation.

In many spiritual practices, cultivating a healthy spiritual heart involves disciplines like meditation, prayer, gratitude, and self-reflection. By nurturing our spiritual heart, we can experience greater emotional intelligence, compassion, and connection with ourselves, others, and the divine.

In summary, the spiritual heart is a vital concept in understanding human nature and our relationship with God. Created in God's image, humans have a heart that reflects God's nature, yet is finite and fleshly, unlike God's infinite and spiritual heart. The Bible distinguishes between the soul and heart, with the soul encompassing the entire person and the heart referring specifically to the spiritual center of emotions, thoughts, and intentions. The spiritual heart, or psuche heart, is the seat of our inner life, connecting us to God, and is responsible for controlling emotions, intuition, conscience, and faith. Nurturing our spiritual heart through disciplines like meditation, prayer, and self-reflection can lead to greater emotional intelligence, compassion, and connection with the divine. Understanding the spiritual heart's role in our lives encourages us to care for and nurture our entire being, acknowledging its interconnected yet distinct aspects, and inviting us to explore the depths of our spiritual heart, where we can experience the divine and cultivate a deeper relationship with our Creator.

12 CHAPTER twelve
Guarding the Heart: The Power of Hiding God's Word Within

In Matthew 15:18-19, Jesus Christ taught a profound lesson about the human heart and its role in shaping our thoughts, words, and actions. He said, "But what comes out of the mouth proceeds from the heart, and this defiles a person. For out of the heart come evil thoughts, murder, adultery, sexual immorality, theft, false witness, slander."

This passage highlights the heart's vulnerability to various influences, predominantly evil ones. Jesus emphasizes that the heart is the source of our thoughts, words, and actions, and it can be easily corrupted by sinful desires and influences. The heart is the seat of our emotions, motivations, and intentions, making it a prime target for evil influences.

The Bible repeatedly warns about the heart's susceptibility to sin and emphasizes the importance of guarding it. Proverbs 4:23 cautions, "Guard your heart above all else, for it determines the course of your life." This verse underscores the heart's role in shaping our lives and the need for vigilance in protecting it from harmful influences.

The heart's vulnerability stems from its ability to be shaped by various factors, including sinful desires, worldly influences, emotional responses, and spiritual forces. Our hearts can be swayed by selfish desires, leading us astray from God's will. The world's values and beliefs can seep into our hearts, corrupting our thoughts and actions. Unchecked emotions like anger, fear, and pride can dominate our hearts, leading to harmful behavior. The Bible warns about the influence of evil spiritual forces that can seek to control our hearts.

To guard our hearts effectively, we must seek God's wisdom and guidance, renew our minds with God's Word, cultivate self-awareness and self-control, surround ourselves with positive influences and supportive community, and practice prayer, meditation, and spiritual disciplines to stay connected with God.

By acknowledging the heart's vulnerability and taking proactive steps to guard it, we can protect ourselves from evil influences and cultivate a heart that reflects God's love, wisdom, and character. Guarding our heart is a continuous process that requires effort, dedication, and reliance on God's grace. Through this process, we can develop a heart that is pure, wise, and filled with God's love, leading us to live a life that honors Him.

But wait a moment! Can we truly guard our hearts without external guidance? Perhaps, but it's a daunting task. This is where our theme scripture comes in: "I have hidden Your word in my heart, so that I might not sin against You" (Psalm 119:11). The portion that resonates with us today is "so that I might not sin against You." David's primary motivation, aside from his love for God's Word, for hiding God's word in his heart is to avoid sinning against Him.

In this verse, David acknowledges the importance of internalizing God's Word to resist temptation and sin. By hiding God's Word in his heart, David is creating a moral compass that guides his thoughts, actions, and decisions. This intentional act allows him to develop a deeper understanding of God's character and ways, recognize and resist sinful patterns and thoughts, cultivate a sense of accountability and reverence for God, and experience the transformative power of God's Word in his life.

In essence, David is saying that guarding our hearts requires more than just personal effort; it requires surrender, humility, and a willingness to be shaped by God's Word. By embracing this truth, we can develop a stronger resistance to sin and grow in our relationship with God.

But we may still have a problem! While memorizing scripture and reciting verses can be a valuable practice, it is essential to recognize that this alone may not be sufficient to thwart the devil's tactics. In 2 Corinthians 3:6, Paul provides insight into the limitations of relying solely on the "letter" of the law. He contrasts the old covenant, based on

THE HIDDEN WORD: EXPLORING THE SECRETS OF THE HEART

the written law, with the new covenant, which is rooted in the Spirit and brings life, freedom, and transformation.

Paul's statement, "The letter kills, but the Spirit gives life," highlights the distinction between mere external compliance with rules and a living, vibrant relationship with God. The "letter" represents the written law, literal interpretation of scriptures, and external rules and regulations. While these may provide a sense of structure and guidance, they can ultimately lead to death and condemnation due to the inevitable failure to meet the standards. This approach can foster legalism, where individuals focus on external compliance rather than inner transformation, leading to pride and self-righteousness.

In contrast, the "Spirit" refers to the transformative power of the Holy Spirit, who brings life by giving believers a new nature and a transformed heart. The Spirit enables individuals to understand and apply scriptures in a way that leads to freedom, joy, and true spiritual life. He produces fruit such as love, joy, and peace, which are evident signs of a vibrant relationship with God.

Paul's emphasis is on the difference between mere external compliance and a living, dynamic relationship with God through the Holy Spirit. He underscores that true spiritual life comes not from following rules, but from the transformative power of the Spirit. This highlights the importance of balancing knowledge of scripture with a deep, personal connection with God, allowing the Spirit to guide and transform individuals from the inside out.

In various Christian denominations, the guided sinner's prayer serves as a powerful expression of faith, guiding individuals to acknowledge their sinfulness, seek forgiveness, and invite Jesus into their lives.

The prayer's words, "Dear God, I know I've sinned and fallen short of Your standards. I repent of my sins and ask for Your forgiveness. I believe that Jesus died on the cross for my sins and rose again to give me new life. I invite You, Jesus, to come into my heart and be my Lord and

Savior. Help me to turn away from my sins and follow You. Thank You for Your love and mercy. Amen," encapsulate the essence of Christian faith.

The most pivotal part of this prayer is the invitation, "I invite You, Jesus, to come into my heart and be my Lord and Savior." This phrase holds profound significance, as it acknowledges Jesus Christ as the Word of God, who was present with God in the beginning and is, in fact, God Himself (John 1:1). The Word, which embodies life and light, shines in the darkness, yet the darkness fails to comprehend it (John 1:4-5).

By inviting Jesus into one's heart, an individual is, in essence, inviting the Word of God into their life. This act of invitation allows the Word to take residence, guiding and transforming the person from within. As the psalmist wrote, "Your word I have hidden in my heart, that I might not sin against You" (Psalm 119:11). By hiding the Word in one's heart, one gives Jesus Christ the better part of their life, allowing His teachings and guidance to shape their thoughts, actions, and decisions.

In this sense, the sinner's prayer is not merely a ritualistic expression but a heartfelt invitation to allow Jesus, the Word of God, to dwell within and transform one's life. As the apostle Paul wrote, "Christ in you, the hope of glory" (Colossians 1:27). By inviting Jesus into our hearts, we open ourselves to His transformative power, allowing Him to become the hope of glory within us.

The concept of hiding the Word of God in one's heart serves as a strategic defense mechanism, aimed at preventing sin and rebellion against God. The heart, being the central hub of human emotions, thoughts, and intentions, is the battleground where good and evil constantly clash. By storing the Word of God in this critical area, an individual effectively places a vigilant guardian, akin to a skilled sniper, who watches for and eliminates potential threats without hesitation.

THE HIDDEN WORD: EXPLORING THE SECRETS OF THE HEART

This clandestine guard, armed with the power of God's Word, patrols the heart's terrain, intercepting and neutralizing harmful thoughts, emotions, and desires before they can take hold and lead to sin. The Psalmist's declaration, "Your word I have hidden in my heart, that I might not sin against You" (Psalm 119:11), underscores the importance of this internal safeguard.

As the Bible teaches, "Above all else, guard your heart, for everything you do flows from it" (Proverbs 4:23). By hiding the Word in one's heart, an individual fortifies this critical stronghold, ensuring that God's truth and wisdom guide their actions, decisions, and relationships. This internalized Word serves as a powerful deterrent against sin, empowering individuals to resist temptation and walk in obedience to God's will.

In essence, hiding the Word of God in one's heart is a proactive measure, establishing a protective barrier that shields against the enemy's tactics and safeguards one's relationship with God. As the apostle Paul wrote, "Take the helmet of salvation and the sword of the Spirit, which is the word of God" (Ephesians 6:17). By hiding this sword in one's heart, an individual equips themselves for spiritual battle, ready to face life's challenges with courage, wisdom, and faithfulness.

Furthermore, precautions are indeed crucial, as the age-old adage reminds us that prevention is better than cure. In Psalm 119:11, David shares a profound reason for hiding God's word in his heart, serving as a precautionary measure: "so that I might not sin against you." By internalizing God's word, David aimed to fortify himself against the temptations and challenges that could lead him astray.

This verse highlights the importance of being proactive in our spiritual lives. By taking preventive measures, we can avoid pitfalls and maintain a strong connection with God. David's approach demonstrates the value of proactive obedience, as he chose to hide

God's word in his heart, taking initiative to align himself with God's will.

David also shows self-awareness, recognizing his own vulnerabilities and taking steps to protect himself from sin. He equipped himself for life's challenges by storing God's word in his heart, ensuring he could draw upon divine guidance when needed. His desire to hide God's word in his heart reveals a deep longing for intimacy and connection with his Creator.

In today's world, we face numerous challenges that can lead us away from God's path. By embracing David's precautionary approach, we can develop a deeper understanding of God's word and its application in our lives. We can cultivate self-awareness, recognizing areas where we need spiritual reinforcement, and fortify ourselves against temptation and sin, relying on God's word as our guide.

By hiding God's word in our hearts, we can follow David's example, taking proactive steps to prevent spiritual pitfalls and maintain a vibrant connection with our heavenly Father. This approach enables us to nurture a stronger, more intimate relationship with God, seeking His guidance and wisdom in all aspects of life.

13 CHAPTER thirteen
Hiding God's Word in Our Hearts: A Journey of Transformation and Devotion

In Psalm 119:11, David's statement "so that I might not sin against you" reveals a humble and contrite heart, seeking guidance and protection from God. David is not boasting about his own righteousness or comparing himself to others, but rather, he is responding to God's call to obedience. He is essentially saying, "Lord, I want to follow Your commandments, but I need Your help. Teach me Your statutes and guide me in Your ways, so that I might not stray from Your path."

David's plea is rooted in his recognition of God's sovereignty and his own frailty. He acknowledges that without God's guidance, he is susceptible to sin and rebellion. By hiding God's Word in his heart, David is seeking to internalize God's truth, but he knows that this is not enough. He needs God's ongoing instruction and protection to navigate life's challenges.

Centuries later, Jesus would echo this sentiment in His teaching on prayer, saying, "Lead us not into temptation, but deliver us from the evil one" (Matthew 6:13). This prayer, often referred to as the Lord's Prayer, reflects the same desire for guidance and protection that David expressed in Psalm 119.

In essence, David is saying, "Lord, I want to follow Your will, but I need Your help. Teach me Your laws, guide me in Your ways, and protect me from sin. I don't want to sin against You, but I know that I can only avoid sin by Your grace and guidance." This prayer demonstrates a deep understanding of human weakness and the need for divine assistance in living a life that honors God.

In Psalm 119, section GIMEL, verse 17, David expresses his heartfelt desire: "Deal bountifully with Your servant, that I may live and keep Your word." David's motivation for keeping God's word is rooted in his understanding of its creative power. He recognizes that

God's Logos, the thought-carrying word, has the ability to bring things into being. This same word, when spoken, becomes Rhema, the spoken word of God, which includes prophecy, revelation, and the powerful sayings of Jesus Christ, whom David believed was present from the beginning.

David also delights in the Graphē (Γραφή), the written word of the LORD, which encompasses the Rhema put into writing. He understands that Logos, Rhema, and Graphē are all interconnected aspects of God's word, originating from the same source - God Himself. These three concepts represent the various ways God communicates with humanity:

- Logos: The thought-carrying word of God, symbolizing God's eternal wisdom and plan.

- Rhema: The spoken word of God, representing God's direct communication with individuals or groups.

- Graphē: The written word of God, comprising the recorded Scriptures that serve as a permanent witness to God's revelation.

Throughout Psalm 119, David weaves together these concepts, demonstrating his comprehensive understanding of God's multifaceted word. By acknowledging the creative power of Logos, the direct communication of Rhema, and the enduring witness of Graphē, David shows his reverence for the various ways God reveals Himself and communicates with humanity.

In the same Psalm, David continues to express his deep longing for God's word, revealing themes of revival, comfort, obedience, understanding, devotion, assurance, and longing.

David's soul clings to the dust, symbolizing spiritual dryness, and he cries out for life according to God's word, seeking revitalization (Psalm 119:25). His soul weeps due to grief, and he asks God to strengthen him according to His word, seeking solace in times of sorrow (verse 28).

THE HIDDEN WORD: EXPLORING THE SECRETS OF THE HEART

He expresses his willingness to follow God's commandments, asking God to enlarge his heart, symbolizing a desire for increased capacity to obey (verse 32). David requests understanding to keep God's law, demonstrating his commitment to obedience (verse 34). He asks God to incline his heart towards His testimonies, seeking a heart focused on God's word rather than worldly gain (verse 36).

David requests God's word to be confirmed to him, seeking assurance in his devotion to God (verse 38). He expresses his deep longing for God's commandments, seeking life in God's righteousness (verse 40).

Throughout these verses, David's love for God's word shines through, revealing his desire for spiritual revival, comfort, obedience, understanding, devotion, assurance, and a deep longing for God's commandments. He recognizes the transformative power of God's word, seeking to be shaped by it in every aspect of his life.

In Section VAU of Psalm 119, David continues to express his deep longing for God's word and His presence in his life. He cries out for God's mercies to come to him, according to His salvation and word, revealing his dependence on God's grace and truth.

David's trust in God's word gives him confidence to respond to those who mock him, demonstrating the defensive power of God's word in the face of opposition. He asks God not to remove the word of truth from his mouth, indicating his desire to continue speaking and proclaiming God's truth, even in challenging circumstances.

David's hope is rooted in God's judgments, signifying his trust in God's justice and righteousness. He recognizes that God's word is a source of strength, guidance, and protection, and he seeks to cling to it in all aspects of his life.

Through these verses, David showcases the importance of trusting in God's word, even when faced with mockery or adversity. He exemplifies the posture of a believer who relies on God's truth to navigate life's challenges, and his desire to continue speaking and proclaiming God's word demonstrates his commitment to sharing the hope and salvation he has found in God.

In Section ZAYIN, David continues to extol the virtues of God's word, emphasizing its life-giving power and comfort in times of affliction. He asks God to remember the word He spoke to His servant, which has become David's hope and comfort.

David testifies that God's word has given him life, highlighting the transformative power of Scripture. This life-giving word is not just a source of comfort but also a beacon of hope in the midst of adversity. As Jesus later affirms, "It is the Spirit who gives life; the flesh profits nothing. The words that I speak to you are spirit, and they are life" (John 6:63).

The word of God, which is life, is also the light of the world. As David writes, "Your word is a lamp to my feet and a light to my path" (Psalm 119:105). This light illuminates the darkness, guiding us through life's challenges and revealing the path of righteousness.

In a world filled with darkness and despair, God's word shines brightly, offering hope and life to all who receive it. David's testimony underscores the importance of clinging to God's word, especially in times of affliction, for it is in this word that we find life, comfort, and guidance. As the apostle John writes, "In Him was life, and the life was the light of men" (John 1:4).

In Section CHETH of Psalm 119, David continues to express his devotion to God's word, highlighting the distinction between "Your words" and "Your word". In verse 57, David declares that God is his portion, and he has committed to keeping God's words, plural. This refers to the collective teachings, commandments, and promises found in Scripture.

In contrast, verse 58 reveals David's desire for God's favor, seeking mercy according to God's word, singular. This singular word represents the unified, cohesive message of God's truth, which encompasses His promises, wisdom, and guidance.

David's distinction between "words" and "word" underscores the importance of understanding the Bible as both a collection of individual teachings and a unified, life-giving message. By keeping God's words, David is committed to obeying His commandments and following His teachings. By seeking mercy according to God's word, David is trusting in the overarching message of God's truth and redemption.

This nuanced understanding of God's word is essential for believers, as it highlights the importance of both individual obedience to God's teachings and trust in His unified message of salvation. As Jesus said, "It is the Spirit who gives life; the flesh profits nothing. The words that I speak to you are spirit, and they are life" (John 6:63). By embracing both the individual words and the unified word of God, believers can experience the fullness of life and mercy that God offers.

In Section TETH of Psalm 119, David continues to extol the virtues of God's word, emphasizing its transformative power and truth. In verse 65, David acknowledges God's goodness in dealing with him according to His word, highlighting the reliability and faithfulness of God's promises.

In verse 67, David reflects on his past, admitting that he strayed from God's path before experiencing affliction. However, through his trials, David has come to keep God's word, demonstrating the refining power of adversity in deepening his commitment to God's truth.

David's testimony underscores the importance of hiding God's word in one's heart, as he writes earlier in Psalm 119:11, "I have hidden Your word in my heart, that I might not sin against You." This intentional act of storing God's word in his heart has enabled David to navigate life's challenges with integrity and faithfulness.

The truth of God's word has become David's anchor, guiding him through affliction and temptation. By embracing this truth, David has experienced the liberating power of God's word, which sets us free from sin's bondage and enables us to walk in obedience to God's will. As

Jesus declares, "If you abide in My word, you are My disciples indeed. And you shall know the truth, and the truth shall set you free" (John 8:31-32).

In Sections JOD and KAPH of Psalm 119, the Psalmist continues to express his deep longing for God's word and His presence in his life. In verse 74, he writes that those who fear God will rejoice when they see him, because he has hoped in God's word. This hope is not just a fleeting feeling but a confident expectation rooted in the truth of God's promises.

In verse 81, the Psalmist's soul faints, or grows weary, as he waits for God's salvation. Yet, he continues to hope in God's word, demonstrating his unwavering trust in God's deliverance. His eyes fail, or grow dim, as he eagerly awaits God's comfort, crying out, "When will You comfort me?" (verse 82).

The Psalmist's desperation is palpable, but his hope remains anchored in God's word. He knows that God's truth is his only source of comfort and strength in the midst of trials. As he writes earlier, "I have hidden Your word in my heart, that I might not sin against You" (Psalm 119:11). This hidden word becomes his lifeline, sustaining him through the darkest of times.

The Psalmist's testimony reminds us that our hope is not in circumstances or human strength but in the unchanging truth of God's word. As the apostle Paul writes, "For whatever things were written before were written for our learning, that we through the patience and comfort of the Scriptures might have hope" (Romans 15:4).

14 CHAPTER fourteen
Embracing Our True Identity: Becoming Sons of God through His Word

Now that we've discovered the significance of hiding God's Word in our hearts, and how to treasure, store, and keep it close, we can draw a profound spiritual conclusion based on biblical truths. When we hide God's Word in our hearts, we're intentionally making it an integral part of our being, allowing it to shape our thoughts, emotions, and actions. We're essentially saying, "God, I want Your Word to be the guiding force in my life, shaping my decisions and directing my path.

As the Psalmist so eloquently expressed, hiding God's Word in our hearts enables us to avoid sinning against Him. Sin, in essence, is anything that separates us from God, anything that contradicts His will. By knowing God's Word, we gain insight into His expectations for us, and we learn how to live a life that pleases Him.

Hiding God's Word in our hearts is a deliberate choice we make every day – a choice to prioritize our relationship with Him, seek His guidance, and live in a way that honors Him. Let us commit to hiding God's Word in our hearts, just as the Psalmist did. Let us treasure it, store it safely, and keep it close. As we do, we'll find ourselves better equipped to live the life God desires for us – a life that is pleasing to Him and fulfilling for us.

Having come to understand who the Logos is and why we need Him in our hearts, we can now embrace the transformative power of His presence in our lives. By hiding God's Word in our hearts, we invite the Logos to dwell within us, guiding us toward a life of purpose, joy, and eternal significance.

After all, hiding God's Word in our hearts is, in essence, hiding Him in our hearts. This act of concealment is not about secrecy, but about safeguarding the precious treasure of God's presence within us. We do this to protect the Word, Life, and Light of God in us from being snatched away by the evil tactics and deceitful schemes of the enemy (Revelation 3:11).

The Word of God in our hearts serves as our divine mandate, guiding us in our thoughts, words, and actions. It is the blueprint for our lives, empowering us to live according to God's purpose and plan. As the apostle Paul wrote, "For as many as are led by the Spirit of God, they are the sons of God" (Romans 8:14).

The Holy Spirit, who dwells within us, is the deposit of God's presence in our lives. We have been bought with a price, and our bodies and spirits belong to God (1 Corinthians 6:19-20). Therefore, we are called to glorify God in every aspect of our being, using our lives as instruments of worship and praise.

By hiding God's Word in our hearts, we are, in essence, internalizing His character, love, and wisdom, allowing them to take root deep within us. This act of concealment enables us to develop a profound understanding of God's nature and ways, gaining insight into His thoughts and intentions. As we do so, we cultivate a stronger, more intimate relationship with Him, built on trust, faith, and love.

Hiding God's Word in our hearts also allows us to receive guidance and wisdom for our lives, navigating life's challenges with confidence and clarity. Moreover, we experience the transformative power of His presence, undergoing a profound metamorphosis that reflects His glory.

Ultimately, as we hide God's Word in our hearts, we shine as radiant lights in a dark world, reflecting God's character, love, and wisdom, and illuminating the path for others to follow. In this way, hiding God's Word in our hearts is not just an act of memorization, but a journey of transformation, where we increasingly become like Him, and His presence shines through us, touching the lives of those around us.

In essence, hiding God's Word in our hearts is about embracing our true identity as children of God, surrendered to His will, and empowered by His Spirit. As we do so, we become beacons of hope, shining forth the radiance of His presence, and fulfilling our mandate to glorify Him in all we do.

As we journey through life, it's essential to remember that we don't belong to ourselves; we belong to God. He created us with His own thought and reason, His Logos, and instilled within us hearts that beat with purpose. Hiding His Word in our hearts isn't merely a personal choice, but a choice aligned with God's will. Though He granted us freedom as moral agents, He expects us to grow into our full potential, like a farmer nurturing seeds to yield a bountiful harvest.

However, some choose not to please the Farmer, and their lives become mere fodder. But let us strive, like David in Psalm 119:11, to hide God's Word in our hearts, that we might not fall short of His glory. With Jesus Christ living within us, our lives become a reflection of His presence. Even those who encounter us can't help but see the radiance of Christ in our eyes.

As we surrender to God's will, His Logos transforms us from the inside out. We become beacons of hope, shining forth the light of Christ in a world desperate for guidance. May we embrace this truth and allow God's Word to take root in our hearts, that we might live a life worthy of His glory. With Jesus as our guide, we'll navigate life's challenges with confidence, and our lives will become a testament to the power of God's transforming love.

After all, discovering a moment and a willingness to hide God's Word in one's heart is a profound indication of having received Him, and subsequently, being granted the privilege of being called sons of God. This distinction is significant, as it elevates our status from merely being children of God to being sons, as described in John 1:10-12. While Christ Himself is often referred to as the Child of God, He is uniquely designated as the Son of God, highlighting the depth of His relationship with the Father.

In biblical context, a child is born, but a son is given, signifying a deliberate act of endowment (Isaiah 9:6). As sons of God, we are not just born into His family but are intentionally given the power and authority that comes with sonship. This transformation is made possible by our willingness to hide God's Word in our hearts, allowing His truth to shape our thoughts, actions, and identities.

As we embrace our sonship, we begin to understand the magnitude of our inheritance and the responsibilities that accompany it. We are no longer just recipients of God's love but also participants in His divine plan, called to reflect His character and extend His kingdom on earth. By hiding God's Word in our hearts, we seal our identity as sons of God, empowered to live a life that honors our Heavenly Father.

15 CHAPTER fifteen
Epilogue

As we bring our discussion to a close, let's take a moment to recap the key points we've explored. We've delved into the significance of hiding God's Word in our hearts, as mentioned in Psalm 119:11, and uncovered its connection to John 1:1-5, which reveals Jesus Christ as the embodiment of God's thoughts and plans. We've examined the importance of understanding the phrase "In the beginning" (Berēshîth) and its role in setting the stage for God's eternal plan. I repeat, the phrase "In the beginning" (Berēshîth) sets the stage for understanding God's eternal plan, representing the divine blueprint for all existence. Jesus, the incarnate Word, is the ultimate revelation from God to humanity, embodying divine nature, wisdom, love, and redemption.

Additionally, we've discussed the intimate relationship between God and the Word (Logos), the unique nature of the Trinity, and the transformative power of God's Word in our lives. The relationship between God and the Word (Logos) is one of eternal communion and mutual indwelling, mirroring the interdependence of the soul and life. Jesus' statement "I and the Father are one" and 1 John 1:1-2 affirm this divine unity.

The Logos and Holy Spirit possess the unique ability to operate independently while maintaining perfect unity with God, akin to a network of computers synchronizing with a central server. This triune relationship enables diverse functions and manifestations while ensuring unity and coherence in divine operations.

John 1:4 says, "In Him was life, and the life was the light of men."

The Bible's concept of life encompasses Zoe (eternal life), Psuche (psychological life), and Bios (biological life). Jesus Christ offers humanity Zoe, transcending physical existence and mortality.

Hiding God's Word in our hearts establishes a protective barrier against the enemy's tactics and safeguards our relationship with God.

David's testimony in Psalm 119 showcases the transformative power of God's word, giving life, comfort, guidance, and protection.

Ultimately, hiding God's Word in our hearts is an intimate and personal act, inviting God's truth to shape our thoughts, emotions, and actions. By embracing God's word, believers can experience the fullness of life, mercy, and freedom that God offers.

Let's take a moment to reflect on these insights and how they can deepen our understanding of God's character and our relationship with Him.

Psalm 119:11
"I have hidden Your word in my heart, so that I might not sin against You."

ABOUT THE AUTHOR

Jaison Ndlovu, born on July 1, 1960, in Guruve, Zimbabwe, grew up in Bharamasvesve, Zhombe, Kwekwe. He is the second child and eldest son of Katazo Amos Magundwane and Resiya Chikwinya. With four sisters and four brothers, he attended Gwesela St Andrew's School, St Martin de Porres, and Ascot Secondary School for his education. He pursued salesmanship at the Union College of South Africa and Religious Studies at Ambassador Bible College. Jaison is married to Susan Ndlovu (nee Mahogo), and they have four sons and two daughters, all of whom are married. Staying at Empress in Zhombe, Zimbabwe, he is an active contributor as a blogger and editor on Wikipedia, and shares video songs and sermons on YouTube.

Milton Keynes UK
Ingram Content Group UK Ltd.
UKHW041314210924
448622UK00001B/57